Crosscurrents / MODERN CRITIQUES

Harry T. Moore, *General Editor*

From Tension to Tonic
The Plays of
EDWARD ALBEE

Anne Paolucci

WITH A PREFACE BY

Harry T. Moore

SOUTHERN ILLINOIS UNIVERSITY PRESS
Carbondale and Edwardsville

FEFFER & SIMONS, INC.
London and Amsterdam

Contents

♥

35671

Preface

In bringing out the hundredth volume in the Crosscurrents/Modern Critiques series, those of us concerned in its development are pleased and proud, not only because of the auspiciousness of the occasion, but also because the book itself is so excellent. It is a study of one of our leading American playwrights, Edward Albee, by one of today's finest commentators on the art of the theater, Anne Paolucci.

Dr. Paolucci is the first teacher to be appointed Research Professor at St. John's University where, besides teaching and writing, she edits the distinguished critical journal, Review of National Literatures. Notice the plural there: Dr. Paolucci is not limited to American literature, but deals with the writings of various countries. Born in Rome (where she was baptized and confirmed in the magnificent church of Santa Maria Maggiore), she came to the United States in childhood and speaks a flawless English. But her use of the language deserves something more than a partly negative compliment: those who turn to the pages of her book will see how lively and creative she is with English prose. And that is only one of the delights of this book.

A graduate of Barnard College, Professor Paolucci went on to take her master's and doctor's degrees at Columbia University. Besides her work at St. John's she has taught at the City College of CUNY, at New York University, and at the universities of Naples and Urbino. Living at the last place, Urbino, was a most useful experience indeed, since it gave her an opportunity to become acquainted with the rather remote Italian town in which, according to Kenneth Clark in his Civilisation series on television (also published as a book), mankind reached one of its highest points of development in the reigns of the Montefeltro family during the Renaissance —the young Raphael was at the ducal court at Urbino, where Piero della Francesca produced some of his finest paintings and Baldassare Castiglione wrote his great and enduring treatise on manners, The Courtier. Dr. Paolucci has had three of her books published at Urbino: a critical commentary (in Italian) on several of Shakespeare's tragedies; A Short History of American Drama; and—this gets us close to the present volume—a study of O'Neill, Arthur Miller, and Albee.

She has also published books in America, including (in 1971) her Classical Influences in Shakespearean Tragedy. In 1962 she collaborated with her husband, Henry Paolucci, on an edition of Hegel on Tragedy, and she has translated Machiavelli. Her work in the theater has not been just theoretical, for she has staged a number of plays, one of them Albee's The Zoo Story, which she produced in Naples in 1967. Professor Paolucci is also a dramatist in her own right; her play The Short Season was performed in Italy and, in the United States, as an "off-Broadway" feature. Her dramatization of the life of Thomas Cromwell, Minions of the Race, is at this writing being considered for production.

This is only a brief summary of the career of the highly talented Dr. Paolucci. We are happy to announce that she is now preparing a book on Pirandello, one of her chief interests, for the Crosscurrents series.

In the present volume she treats Albee more thoroughly and deeply than anyone before her has done, taking the plays up for serious consideration and showing Albee's inherent Americanism while at the same time revealing his similarities to some of the French writers of the school known as the Absurd. Indeed, with her background, Professor Paolucci is able to see Albee in world perspective. If she now and then invokes such authors as Dante, she is not attempting to intimate that Albee is on a level with Dante—rather, she is quite properly indicating how many Dantean concepts have come through to us.

This book will prove invaluable for students of American literature and particularly for students of American drama, or, for that matter, for all modern drama. And, once again, as our hundredth volume, this book is warmly welcomed into the Crosscurrents/Modern Critiques series. And—we look forward to the Pirandello.

HARRY T. MOORE

Southern Illinois University
November 11, 1972

Acknowledgments

I wish to thank the following publishers:

Atheneum Publishers have granted permission to quote from the following plays by Edward Albee: *Who's Afraid of Virginia Woolf?* Copyright © 1962 by Edward Albee; *Tiny Alice* Copyright © 1965 by Edward Albee; *A Delicate Balance* Copyright © 1966 by Edward Albee; and from the author's introduction to *Box* and *Quotations from Chairman Mao Tse-Tung* Copyright © 1968, 1969 by Edward Albee.
All rights, including professional, amateur, motion picture recitation, lecturing, public reading, radio and television broadcasting are strictly reserved to the author and publisher.

Jonathan Cape Ltd. has granted The British Commonwealth and Empire permission to quote from the following plays by Edward Albee: *Who's Afraid of Virginia Woolf? Tiny Alice, A Delicate Balance,* and Edward Albee's introduction to *Box.*

Coward-McCann, Inc. has granted permission to quote from the plays *The Death of Bessie Smith* © 1959, 1960 by Edward Albee and *The American Dream* © 1960 and 1961 by Edward Albee.

Introduction

This book is the summary of a long, brooding enjoyment of Albee's plays and was written with the presumptuous intention of sharing that enjoyment with others. For this reason, I have pursued no theses or formal patterns of criticism—though I believe Albee's plays are substantial enough in content and form to withstand the most rigorous varieties of critical analysis. I agree with Albee, however, that there is still time, in his case, for impatience with critical labels, with "weighing" new methods "against more familiar ones" whose main virtue is simply that they already exist. And, beyond that, it seems to me that a critic's primary obligation in dealing with a still productive author is to facilitate an appreciative as well as a critical reading of his text.

Of course, it is when we try to be least rigorous, most spontaneous, that our thinking is most apt to let itself be dominated by our cultural habits. My references to other works and authors—Dante, especially—have not been inadvertent, however. At the risk of appearing naïvely prejudiced, I have indulged several times in comparisons with the method and artistic goals of the author of *The Divine Comedy* for the reason that I am convinced that Albee has done more than any other recent author to revive the glorious tradition of polysemous writing, in a modern vein.

I have tried, in other words, to "experience" the plays in writing—as I have already and many times experienced them in reading and in talking about them—following Albee's own suggestion that we "relax and let the plays happen." And because Albee's novelty can best be appreciated where the demands of original content and original form come together, I have excluded from consideration in this book his dramatic adaptations of novels and other plays.

The idea of setting down some of my thoughts on the subject was first suggested to me by my students in American drama at the University of Naples, with whom I shared many of the arguments here set forth, as they took shape. The interest shown in my lectures on one or more of the plays at other universities in Italy and at the University of Innsbruck during 1965, 1966, 1967, confirmed me in my original purpose—as did, also, the reception accorded my production of *The Zoo Story*, sponsored by USIS and The American Studies Center of Naples, in 1967. To these agencies and to the many friends and colleagues who encouraged me in the writing of this book, I wish to express my sincere thanks; to Edward Albee, my equally sincere apologies for presuming to explain—while he is barely past the middle of his journey—what, in the last analysis, can only be felt.

ANNE PAOLUCCI

New York City
1971

From Tension to Tonic

1

The Discipline of Arrogance

All art, said Goethe, is a gesture of arrogance. When it is new it must have the nerve, the sheer brazenness, the courage even, to make room for itself in a crowded tradition. It must come on with a confident sweep, asserting its own superiority, insisting that yesterday has had it and must give ground.

Of course, what is announced as an inspired novelty often proves, in the working out, a pitiful stammering. The defiant gesture that breaks with the past too often carries the artist ahead of his talent so that his own chief resource of strength is lost in the gesture. Which is to say that while art must be arrogant in the confidence of its inspiration, that inspiration cannot be fittingly embodied without the skill and fluency that comes with practice in an art form (what Dante called *usus*), without the knowledge of the medium itself (*ars*), and without the innate talent which gives the stamp of personality to the result (*ingenium*). Without these three prerequisites, the arrogance of inspiration collapses into something foolish and inarticulate. History bears witness to this. The avant-garde exists in every age; and in every age it has had a foolish and inarticulate fringe, whose arrogance, nevertheless, provides the self-confident atmosphere conducive to art. Such a fringe clears the way ahead, but the true artist pauses to look back before taking possession of the ground thus cleared.

Today's avant-garde theater has such a fringe in those who see the future of dramatic art as spontaneous expression, with or without words, "happenings" (recent "demonstrations" might be included here), dramatizations which defy form and make no distinction between audience and spectator, meaning and non-meaning, words and sounds. There is a place—or, rather, a place has obviously been made—for happenings, for "open" theater, for political confrontations and dramatic marches punctuated by symbolic gestures and prepared slogans; but if theater is to remain theater, such impulses must be harnassed and controlled. They cannot ever replace what T. S. Eliot called "the third voice of poetry."

But the threat is not really serious; theater will not be destroyed, no matter how popular happenings or spontaneous dramatizations become. The worst that can happen is that avant-garde critics will make a fetish of novelty for a while, mistaking arrogance (the initial thrust) for greatness and relevancy, condemning ordered genius for its adherence to the standard prerequisites of theater. The avant-garde, for example, may blast the author of *Who's Afraid of Virginia Woolf?* and *Tiny Alice* as old-fashioned for submitting to the traditional conventions of a proscenium stage and a printed text; but such criticism will not hurt Albee in the long run, any more than it has hurt Shakespeare or Pirandello. Albee will survive the craze even as he has survived criticism leveled at him from the opposite extreme, by steady playgoers who find his work difficult and abstract.

Passing between Scylla and Charybdis, at once new and traditional, Albee has succeeded in giving repeatable theatrical expression on many levels to experiences that have for him as well as for his audience all the arrogance of inexplicable happenings. He has often been asked to *explain* his plays and has consistently refused to do so, with insolent assurance in his own worth; he has gained a kind of notorious popularity, but has not given in to the conventions of big-money theater. If anything, his plays get more difficult and his self-confidence more irritating—not because he enjoys frustrating his audience or is contemptuous of them, but because he is exploring, with the brazenness of the confident innovator, new areas of human experience with totally new dramatic means.

Albee is the only playwright, after O'Neill, who shows real growth, the only one who has made a serious effort to break away from the "message" plays which have plagued our theater since O'Neill. Experimentation, for Albee, is a slow internal transformation of the dramatic medium, not an arbitrary exercise in expressionism, or Freudian symbolism, or stream of consciousness. His arrogance is not an empty gesture. He is the only one of our playwrights who seems to have accepted and committed himself to serious articulation of the existential questions of our time, recognizing the incongruity of insisting on pragmatic values in an age of relativity. Dramatic "statement," as Ibsen defined it, through realism, is no longer effective in such an age as ours. Albee has taken on the challenge as no one else in the American contemporary theater has. His work is a refreshing exception to John Gassner's judgment that our theater—with its message plays and its outgrown realism—is in a state of "protracted adolescence" which gives it a "provincial air."

"Happenings" are the extreme reaction to our fossilized theater and play an important role in trimming away the deadwood; Albee represents the first sober attempt to effect a transformation at the core. He has given arbitrary experimentation direction and purpose.

Even in his one-act plays, Albee is avant-garde only in the most serious sense of the word. He brings to our theater something of the poetic experience of Beckett and Ionesco—the same striving for a new dramatic language to fit the shifting scene, the same concern with making use of the stage as an articulate medium which reflects the contemporary condition—in the way, for example, that Italian film makers (Fellini and Antonioni especially) have revolutionized film techniques and raised their medium to a new art. Albee's arrogance as an innovator is prompted by profound artistic instincts which are constantly at work reshaping dramatic conventions. He does not discard such conventions altogether, but restructures them according to the organic demands of his dramatic themes. For Albee there is no a priori commitment to either a specific content or form. His early plays, for instance, reflect simultaneously the fascination of social drama and the effort to overcome that fascination. The later plays struggle head-on with the existential dilemma of our day and the frustrating search for meaning. The effort to define new content corresponds on every level to the search for original and adequate form.

Albee's procedure may be summed up as a kind of *dialectic*, an oscillation between the prosaic and the absurd, obvious and mysterious, commonplaces and revelation. What holds these extremes together as fluid, articulate reality is Albee's refusal to settle for "facts" as we know them, or experience as we have grown accustomed to defining it. A lesser artist might have been tempted to insert the latest "gimmicks" to create an impact; but Albee, with the arrogance and certainty of genius, starts confidently from scratch each time, searching out the spontaneous particular idiom that will do justice to the particular idea. He is the best product to date of the "theater of the absurd" (not excluding the French dramatists who launched it). He has absorbed from the French playwrights all there is to absorb—the Ionesco-like fragmentation of a language no longer functional, the Beckett-like economy of plot, the symbolic suggestions of Adamov, the raw exposures of Genet, the sensitive portraits of Giraudoux. His real master is not O'Neill, who provided the initial impulse for better things in our theater (without the organic principle which would guarantee his innovations, unfortunately), but Pirandello. Like the author of *Six Characters in Search of an Author* and *Right You Are!*, Albee has caught the feverish contradictions of the modern spirit, building from the inside out. And like the best representatives of the absurd tradition, he has discovered that the stage itself must be made articulate, often as a contrast against which the spoken word derives its meaning. His search for a new dramatic language is part of a deep-rooted instinct to find adequate expression for the existential dilemma at the heart of the modern experience.

In this context, social drama and the absolutes it insists on are hopelessly dated. O'Neill himself saw the danger early in his career and abandoned The Provincetown Players when he realized that they were out to "preach" social and political reform. Today that kind of theater serves a sophisticated propaganda program which has much else besides art on its agenda.

Albee's daring techniques and novel language go beyond social commentary to the disease of contemporary life. He has probed deeper than most other American playwrights for the implications of our moral and spiritual exhaustion; and if his originality has not been properly appreciated, it is because American audiences have not been properly trained to recognize either the new idiom or the pessimistic conclusion it tries to articulate. I do not suggest that the burden of dramatic communication lies with the audience; but an audience trained in humanitarian platitudes is not prepared to make the minimal effort required. The difficulty of the content must be accepted before one can begin to appreciate the extraordinary appropriateness of the way it has been portrayed on stage.

From the point of view of the conventional "concerned human being," repudiation of *assertion* and *statement* may seem to be a narcissistic self-indulgence; but in fact what appears atomistic and arbitrary in Albee is simply the organic restructuring of a reality which is no longer effective. The transformation is difficult but not new; it caught on long ago in painting, music, and poetry. In drama, the French alone have explored its rich possibilities deliberately and with success. This exploration is long overdue in the American theater.

Albee is the first playwright in the American theater to capture the feverish contradictions of our age, translating communication as commonly understood and accepted into a polarization of opposites, a skeptical questioning of "facts," substituting irony for statement and paradox for simplistic optimism. His cutting sarcasm is, understandably, one of his greatest achievements.

The main difficulty in this kind of theater lies in finding the proper balance, on stage, between dialogue and inanimate objects made articulate, between conscious awareness and unconscious suggestion. Antonioni's films are perhaps the extreme expression of the attempt to make the details surrounding conscious life speak out. The camera moves among objects like an insistent voice, underscoring, denying, outlining, setting up a silent opposition to conventional and recognizable events. Whatever the ultimate value of his technique, it serves extremely well to point up the *kind* of language demanded by an existential premise. On the stage, such a technique naturally must be corrected; drama has its own special demands. The playwright is restricted by the physical, immediate unity of the stage and the impossibility of using close-ups or of letting the camera move instead of the protagonists. He must find other ways to make the physical surroundings speak for him. O'Neill was the first of our dramatists to sense the need for such contrasts. In *All God's Chillun' Got Wings*, for example, his stage directions call for a contracting set—an ambitious design for any dramatist! Albee has turned the very limitations of the stage to his advantage. The most impressive example of the creation of a new *absurd* dimension on stage is the giant replica of the mansion in *Tiny Alice*, the most effective use to date of backdrop as dramatic script—not excluding Ionesco's empty chairs, his expanding creature of dead love, the recording machine in Beckett's *Krapp's Last Tape*. Albee has surpassed his teachers in this technique. His use of stage props—from *Tiny Alice* to *Box*—is intimate and discursive, not mere background or sheer experimentation, but living dialogue which expands as awareness increases. Perhaps the most intriguing and ambitious of these "props" is the dying man in *All Over*. The Unseen Patient, who had been kept alive in the hospital with tubes and transfusions (but who seemed, instead, to be keeping the medical gadgets alive), is the source of life for the people gathered in the room where he lies. He is the heartbeat of the dramatic action; the others nearby are "wired" into him like the TV cameras downstairs and the audience itself are "wired" into the action. This simple but expanding conceit more than makes up for the dialogue of the play, which in its lines is perhaps the least suggestive of all Albee's works; the dying man pumps meaning and unity into the larger scenes, giving them added literary dimension. As originally staged, the backstage apparatus of ropes and wires was left visible on both sides of the isolated set to extend the range of the conceit still further.

It is not without significance that, in spite of his personal commitment to certain popular causes, Albee has resisted the lure of social drama and the language of assertion. He seems to sense the artistic danger of indulging in the kind of writing which O'Neill described as "beyond theater," and which Ionesco labeled in his notebooks on drama as "one dimensional." The political and social realities of any age will find their way into art, of course; but the artist cannot indulge in personal crusades. If we still enjoy Aristophanes's *Clouds*, it is not because we identify with the social critic of Athens and side with him against this or that man, but because the dramatist in him was stronger than the reformer and produced a masterpiece.

Part of the trouble here lies with our critics, who encourage the *committed* play. According to one such critic, theater must be "subversive" to have dramatic impact. Even Arthur Miller, who is as much critic as playwright, is convinced that greatness in drama is the direct result of ethical commitment and of the playwright's acceptance of his role as moral arbiter and judge. Miller has said time and again that the tragic view of life is all-important, but that it is possible only where individual responsibility is recognized. Right and wrong, moral order, *blame*, are the values on which tragedy is built. We must struggle, says Miller, to insist on such values because where no order is believed in, no order can be breached—and thus all disasters of man will strive vainly for moral meaning. For Miller, "a true tragic victory may be scored" * once again, provided we recover the notion of a "moral law" † of individual re-

---

* Robert Hogan, *Arthur Miller* (Minneapolis: University of Minnesota Press, 1964), p. 9.

† Arthur Miller, "Tragedy and the Common Man," *Modern Drama*, ed. Anthony Caputi (New York: W. W. Norton, 1966), pp. 329–30.

sponsibility as opposed to "the purely psychiatric view of life" or "the purely sociological." He insists that "if all our miseries, our indignities, are born and bred within our minds, then all action, let alone the heroic action, is obviously impossible." *

The principle is commendable in itself—and when a true artist is inspired by it (as Miller unquestionably was in the early plays), it cannot fail to produce commendable results. Unfortunately, the committed writer is often too ready to mold his medium to suit his compelling message and to identify with one side against the other. Where the audience is committed in the same way, such a play may even take on the semblance of artistic success. But, as Eric Bentley has keenly observed, innocence—especially for an artist—is suspect and misleading. The dramatist must be constantly alert to the dangers of simplistic moral extremes. The guilty may indeed be black with guilt, but the innocent are never wholly free from the burden of responsibility. In any case, the stage is not the place for such judgments, especially when they threaten to force the dramatic medium to serve an end which is something other than art.

Albee has never succumbed to the temptation of using the stage for indignant social commentary. Even in his early plays (the external "frame" of *The Death of Bessie Smith* is a fine example of such temptation to moralize), he never actually betrays his characters by reducing them to expressions of *guilt* and *innocence*. His most negative portrayals are handled with sympathetic insight into the complex totality of human motivation. In his hands, the polemic against the American family becomes a commentary on all human relationships, his violent anti-clericalism turns into a provocative question about salvation and faith, his bit-

* Ibid. See also Alan Downer, *Recent American Drama* (Minneapolis: University of Minnesota Press, 1961), pp. 34–35.

ing criticism of racial intolerance is transformed into a
subtle analysis of human insufficiency. The social problems he has inherited from our one-dimensional dramatic tradition are never resolved as dogmatic confrontations. In spite of his insolence, his harsh and often
puerile judgments, his bitter sarcasm, Albee is irresist-
ibly drawn to the profound skepticism of the absurd.

This skepticism reaches its limits, on the stage, in the
tendency toward dissolution of character. Like all the
other difficulties connected with the theater of the absurd, it rests on a paradox and a contradiction. Drama
is action (though not necessarily plot as commonly understood), and action presupposes characters to carry
it out, and characters must make themselves understood
if the audience is to share in the experience the dramatist has articulated. The theater of the absurd has
struggled to find ways of redefining these essentials,
juxtaposing internal *landscape* and external events, facts
and fantasy, reshaping language to suit the splintered
action, using everything the stage offers to do so. But
the kind of protagonist that emerges within this new
medium is forever threatening to dissolve into a voice,
a mind, a consciousness, a strange creature without
identity or personality. Dramatists like Sartre and Ca-
mus have skillfully shifted attention away from the
difficulty; their characters remain organically whole, integrated and unified by the internal law of individuality.
The problem, however, does not cease to exist because
it is masked. It is, without a doubt, the most immediate
and pressing problem of the contemporary theater, but
its history is at least as old as *Hamlet*.

In the most modern of his heroes, Shakespeare almost
lets go of dramatic personality as understood from the
time of the Greeks, threatening to destroy it at the core.
Character is reduced to irreconcilable levels of consciousness—as the unusual effect of the soliloquies

makes clear. These stand out from the surrounding action like islands of an internal life which seems often unrelated to the intentions professed by the hero and the actions which result from such intentions. What emerges is a surrealistic mosaic of human impulses, an internal world which remains inviolate in spite of tumultuous external events. The sensitive Hamlet of the soliloquies and the Machiavellian prince capable of sending his best friends to death on mere suspicion is a double image which is never sharpened into a single focus. The audience's response is strangely dependent on the soliloquies; it is detached from the facts of the action. We remember the character as seen from *within*, and the action of the play remains somewhat distant and unreal. We follow the play through the paradoxical psychology of the strange hero who strips his consciousness bare before us.

Modern psychoanalysis and the popularization of Freud have made the notion of unresolved impulses and the subconscious a commonplace; its implications for the stage, however, have yet to be explored meaningfully—although the history of dramatic innovation clearly points to such an examination. To grasp something of what has taken place, one need only compare the sculpturelike creations of Greek drama—exquisitely molded according to their fixed purpose—with the characters of Pirandello or Beckett or even the partly realized, rough-hewn attempts of O'Neill in such plays as *Strange Interlude* (Nina) or *The Great God Brown* (Dion, Brown), or the Greek-inspired figures in *Mourning Becomes Electra* (Lavinia, Orin, Ezra).

Hamlet marks the turning point; and it is not farfetched to say that Goldoni first showed the possibilities of modern character delineation in his whimsical and wholly arbitrary treatment of secondary figures. But the first to assume the challenge as an important and conscious innovation, and to succeed in the attempt, was Pirandello. His characters are indeed *maschere nude*—stripped semblances of what is commonly called "character." What makes the Pirandellian experience a giant step forward, dramatically, is not simply the playwright's insistence on the fragmentation of personality at the core, but his way of going about it. We see the integrated or seemingly integrated character collapse in slow stages before our eyes through an ever more intense oscillation between what *is* and what *appears to be*; between acknowledged purpose and hidden intentions; between the outer shell of life and the living truth which resists all *facts*. Human personality is subtly transformed, even as we watch, into instinct, revelation, doubt, confession, assertion, denial. Action is translated into shifting points of motivation, contradictory statements arranged into a spiral of events, each somehow containing the life of the whole, like the seed which contains the physical potential of the human being. Naturally, action too will appear fragmented in this sort of scheme; the immediate moment is everything. It's hard to say, after seeing or reading a Pirandello play, just what this or that person really is; but we know quite well what he thinks, feels, suffers. We seem to be inside looking out. To concentrate on the *facts* of the action is to lose the heartbeat of the Pirandellian world, the living mask.

In more recent drama—Ionesco might be cited as an example—the dangers of this tendency begin to make themselves felt. The dissolution of character, if carried far enough, must destroy the very notion of character—just as the destruction of conventional language threatens to destroy the possibility of dramatic communication. Pushed to extremes, the dissolution of character takes on the appearance of *types*, on one hand, and *symbols*, on the other—ready-made clichés and enigmatic representations. The protagonists of *The Sand-box* and *The American Dream* point up the danger in Albee's plays—but even in these "experimental" pieces the crotchety old women, the submissive males, the frighteningly efficient females, have their own individual charm as dramatic characters. In *Tiny Alice* Albee proves that he has overcome the danger. Like the Dantesque figures who express themselves simply and directly in the characteristic *act* which sums up their existence, Albee's protagonists are beautifully realized in their single purpose as independent creations made infinitely suggestive through a shocking and utterly transparent allegory. *Box* is, in this respect, a transcendent tour de force.

In his genial answer to the dissolution of character, as in his bold new techniques to reduce action to a transparency and language to ironic paradox, Albee has given ample evidence of his mastery of the dramatic medium. He is the arrogant newcomer who has challenged our seemingly impregnable commitment to social drama and forced us to terms, stripping familiar pragmatic conclusions to provocative questions and the mask of personality down to its mysterious pulse. Not since the time of O'Neill has the American theater witnessed such a confident assertion of artistic arrogance.

2

The Existential Burden
The Death of Bessie Smith, The Sandbox,
The American Dream, The Zoo Story

If one were to sum up Albee's contribution to the American stage, the immediate answer would surely have to be: his language. There is nothing in our theater to compare with the verbal pyrotechnics of *Who's Afraid of Virginia Woolf?*, with the structured but transparent symbolism of *Tiny Alice,* with the compelling story-telling technique found in *The Zoo Story* and *A Delicate Balance.*

From the very beginning—and culminating in *Box* —Albee has proved himself a master of dialogue. He has, in fact, revolutionized the language of the American stage, extending verbal metaphor into the visual settings of his plays, working isolated ironic meanings into a complex network of interrelated ironic reverberations, and using epic topography to maintain allegorical simplicity. He has elaborated conversation with a sensitive ear to its complex musical effects (fugues, partitas, lyrical arias, nervous recitatifs), moving easily from major to minor moods, matching harmonic shifts with subtle tone changes from *largo maestoso* to *pianissimo,* heightening meaning with sudden reversals in style, juxtaposing cliché with pompous rhetoric, slang with archaic formality, hysterical fluency with monosyllabic exhaustion, establishing a variety of rhythms which are a constant surprise within the simple framework of the action. All of this, by itself, is a great achievement; but it does not, all by itself, explain adequately Albee's greatness.

Albee's dramatic language traces a pattern and a purpose which change with each play but which can be summed up generally as a commitment to expose and condemn everything that has been taken for granted for so long. There is something very personal about his social diatribe and in the leveling which results: nothing and no one is spared. But Albee is not a reformer like Arthur Miller or LeRoi Jones. He is not out to correct social injustice or to improve family relationships or to propose a solution to the emptiness of material prosperity. With the true instinct of the artist, he transforms social diatribe into an existential question; like Pirandello, he is not satisfied with exposing the public image but works his way into the private conscience, stripping it bare. The energy of the reformer is all there, but directed into very different channels. He is not a critic with an ideal set of values but the Promethean destroyer of modern myths.

The social themes are apt to mislead us, as in *The Death of Bessie Smith*, *The American Dream*, *The Sandbox*, *The Zoo Story*, *A Delicate Balance*, and *All Over*. (It is only fair to note that where the plays have been well received, it has been to a large measure due to social themes.) The audience that could accept *The Death of Bessie Smith* finds itself hopelessly lost in *Tiny Alice*, where the social diatribe turns into a metaphysical question right before our eyes. The early play allowed for a neat pragmatic solution, even though the author did not spell it out; but *Tiny Alice* forces us to deny the very possibility of a solution. The first scene of the play, whatever its social message, is soon forgotten in the larger context; and by the end, the critical focus—if we insist on it—has shifted drastically. In the wake of Albee's pitiless attack, nothing and no one emerges unscathed. The bad guys elude all attempts at labeling; and the good guys emerge as monstrous frauds. What might seem in the accepted jargon a contradiction is in fact inexorable dialectic.

There is no philosophical pretense in all this, but the method is fundamentally Socratic. The daimon which insists on stripping away the façade of daily existence with stinging, purposeful precision is not unlike the daimon which possessed Socrates and drove him into self-righteous obstinacy. In the Socratic manner, Albee sustains his position at the expense of moderation and tact. His negative stoicism resembles the extremism of the martyr.

The method is Socratic even to the paradoxical affirmation which finally emerges. Socrates's incisive probing was not meant to undermine the universals but to correct the manner of accepting them; but in insisting on the authority of his own private conviction, he set up a new authority at once arbitrary and personal which made his criticism understandably suspect in the eyes of others. Albee has pretty much the same effect on his audience. His quarrel, ultimately, is with absolutes as such; and in demolishing them, he necessarily raises his own judgment to an absolute. Negation turns into an existential assertion which restricts his vision. The paradox forces itself upon us with sharp insistence; it is especially irritating because—in spite of the philosophical implications—Albee is not given to philosophic consistency. His temperament is essentially unphilosophic and—as the critic Lee Baxandall ("The Theatre of Edward Albee," *Tulane Drama Review*, 1965, pp. 19–40) has observed—makes for an "unconscious acceptance of some attributes of that very consensus he scorns in other respects." Although incapable of "historical affirmations," he often falls into them and loses himself in "cliché cynicisms." Albee's power lies in the recognition of the difficulty and in his almost perverse refusal to trim it down to a direct and acceptable statement.

The clearest of these unconscious affirmations is in *The Death of Bessie Smith*. On the surface, the play bears a curious resemblance to the old *moralities*: Nurse is the embittered, evil-possessed villain; her father, even worse (but since he has little impact on the action of the play, his part is less significant); Orderly is the symbol of impotence, the undecided Negro torn between subservience to his enemies and self-respect; Intern is the undecided white, torn between small responsibility and large ideals. There is nothing to counteract properly the evil forces in the play; not until *Tiny Alice* is a respectable equivalent finally defined to offset the forces of corruption.

As compelling social drama, *The Death of Bessie Smith* fails on two counts: the opposing sides of the contest are unevenly matched, and the *tragic* issue lacks emotional immediacy. Jack and Bessie (who is never seen or heard to speak), mere shadows to begin with, are thrown into even deeper obscurity by the ambiguous figure of Nurse, by far the most interesting and articulate figure in the play. Jack—the symbol of naïve, unsuspecting goodness—is simply a target for Nurse's frustrated sense of authority, but Nurse herself is anything but a symbol. She is a curious mixture of motives, a victim of her own psychological contradictions. The fascination she exerts throws everyone else into insignificance.

If a dramatic conflict exists at all, it is not between Jack and Nurse—the death of Bessie is in every sense peripheral to the main action of the play—but between Nurse and Orderly, the light-skinned Negro who works in the hospital. Even this contrast is uneven, however; Orderly is no match for Nurse's sadistic mocking. All his attempts to assert his dignity are vain. Still, of all the characters in the play, he is perhaps the most successful from a purely dramatic point of view; certainly, he is the most consistent and the easiest to identify. His motivations are always clear, even though they are more often implied than stated; where they are defined, it is Nurse who defines them. Whether or not the things she ascribes to him are true is not important; everything he does and says fits the picture she sketches for us. He is awed by the Mayor's presence in the hospital and hopes to talk to him about a better job—and is not at all abashed when the Mayor answers his greeting by shouting, "My ass hurts, you get the hell out of here!" His lines throughout the play are broken or unfinished phrases; he is unequal to his aspirations. Nurse confuses him with her open contempt, but never really succeeds in angering him; after weak denials and poor attempts at remonstrances, he gives in each time—to the point of running out to get her cigarettes, early in the play, and echoing her words and aligning himself with her against his own people, at the end. The stage directions for his last speech—"his back to the wall"—sum up the man beautifully. Whether or not he really bleaches his skin at night, to make it lighter, is irrelevant; psychologically, he betrays himself in everything he does and says. Nurse's estimate is painfully correct: "you are a genuine ass-licker, if I ever saw one."

Nurse is the demonic voice of reality that gives shape to the confusion around her. She strips bare the contradictions in her lover with the same merciless probing characteristic of her exchanges with Orderly. With Intern, however, she doesn't come to the point at once.

Their personal relationship acts as a deflector for a while. She indulges herself with conversation inspired for the most part by a kind of prurient lust. She allows him to skirt obscenely around other subjects, enjoying the sex talk and urging him on coyly. He picks up the cue each time, propositioning her, proposing to her, appealing to that side of her that loves to tell and hear dirty jokes and to indulge in violent necking. He claims to love her, but there is no suggestion of love in anything he does and says, just as there is nothing in her to inspire love. Occasionally, the talk turns to other things —it is Nurse, usually, who takes the initiative—such as his frustrated hope to fight and work where it really counts, presumably in oppressed Spain, but it always comes back to Sex. Intern finally arouses her implacable hatred by reminding her that she has given others what she denies him. She vows to "get him," with an intensity which is disproportionate to the apparent cause; under her merciless attack, Intern, like Orderly, is forced on the defensive. Both waver before her; both are destroyed in the confrontation.

Motivation, as commonly understood, is the weak point of the play; but to stop here means to miss the dramatic novelty of this early work. Language, though cleverly handled, is not yet the brilliant, sharp weapon it becomes in the later plays—although Nurse's remarks already suggest something of the hysterical fluency of *Who's Afraid of Virginia Woolf?* What is striking about the play is the violence it betrays—a violence wholly inexplicable in terms of surface causes. Intern's reminder that he is probably the only white man under sixty in two counties who has not had the pleasure of making love to her—even if just a rumor—cannot really come as a shock to Nurse. Her own father has accused her in much more brutal terms. Her hostility to Intern seems exaggerated, especially since she has turned down his proposal. Her feelings are hard to sort out properly into meaningful motivation; they are often contradictory. She is willing, for example, to reverse herself completely, in Intern's case, from the stand she had assumed with Orderly, encouraging her lover to do the very thing she had mocked the Negro for wanting to do: approach the Mayor and ingratiate himself.

The irony of her reversal is typical of the dialectic of the absurd. It warns us against neat *statement* both in the obvious cause-and-effect relationships and in the subconscious explanations. There are many such warnings. In the same scene, Intern—rising for a moment to something like heroic stature in response to Nurse's bitter tauntings—betrays in the idealism he professes the very weakness which Nurse has come to recognize in him.

> My dissatisfactions . . . you call them that . . . my dissatisfactions have nothing to do with loyalties. . . . I am not concerned with politics . . . but I have a sense of urgency . . . a dislike of waste . . . stagnation . . . I am STRANDED . . . HERE. . . . My talents are not large . . . but the emergencies of the emergency ward of this second-rate hospital in this second-rate state . . . No! . . . it isn't enough. . . . If I could . . . bandage the arm of one person . . . if I could be over there right this minute . . . you could take the city of Memphis . . . you could take the whole state . . . and don't forget I was born here . . . you could take the whole goddam state. . . .

The outburst justifies, ironically, Nurse's scruples. No doubt she too is part of the "second-rate" setup which he is willing to give up for a chance to really do something *grand*, à la Hemingway. Nurse pulls him up short with her brutal response and forces him back to his second-rate reality. Within the narrow limits he has accepted, there is no place for grand displays of sacrifice. Or rather, he falls short of true sacrifice in his self-righteousness. In his complaints he comes very close to Orderly, who also thought he could betray the reality to which he has given tacit approval. Intern's last minute "redemption" at the end of the play—in insisting on doing what is *right*—is as grotesque as Orderly's acceptance of the white man's rules. There can be no escape from self-imposed limits. Heroic stands cannot assume tragic proportions in those who do not know their limitations. The self-sacrificing mood produces only an empty gesture.

With both men, Nurse brings on the confrontation and forces them to reveal themselves in their weakness. But what makes her the most interesting character in the play is the fact that she too is a victim of that same predicament and is forced to take a stand, exposing her own weakness. In her case, the confrontation is implicit, of course, since unlike the men, she never loses sight of either the limitations of her environment or her own contradictory impulses. Her outbursts, like her apathy, reflect a deep psychological awareness which has no adequate expression in conventional terms. She *feels* the trap and knows that no amount of wishful thinking can free her. When she breaks with Intern (at her own instigation) her frustration is vented on Orderly, who happens on the scene at that moment. She taunts him with the suggestion that he would make a much better suitor for her, giggles as Orderly squirms under her sarcastic comment that he go to the Mayor and tell him "that when his butt's better we have a marrying job for him," brings him to the edge of resentment, and insults him mercilessly when he retreats instead into a show of deference. Frustrated even in this petty scheme, Nurse finally turns against herself.

I am SICK. I am sick of everything in this hot, stupid, fly-ridden WORLD. I am sick of the disparity between

things as they are, and as they should be! . . . I am sick
of this desk . . . this uniform . . . the sight of YOU
. . . of him . . . of the smell of Lysol . . . of going to
bed . . . of waking up . . . I am tired . . . of the truth
. . . and I am tired of lying about the truth . . . I am
tired of my skin . . . I WANT OUT!

Her outburst, unlike Intern's, is not against external
causes, but against the internal dilemma over which she
has no control. There is no ideal situation to dream
about, no place where things will be better, no escape.
She alone has grasped this truth.

It is at this moment that Jack bursts in to announce
that he has brought the Negro singer Bessie Smith into
the emergency ward of the white hospital. As a struc-
tural climax, the moment is not altogether satisfactory;
Jack's story is simply a badly constructed frame for
Nurse's story. The two remain unrelated dramatically;
one is simply an arbitrary setting for the resolution of
Nurse's personal difficulties. The social message of the
play is forced back into the action at this point; but
what is missing in dramatic structure is compensated
for in emotional tension. Nurse's stand against admitting Negroes into the hospital brings about her bitter
affirmation of the insoluble condition she herself represents. Her public denunciation of Intern is a confession
as well as a threat; her show of authority, an impatient
reminder that she, at least, entertains no wild schemes
about escaping the trap in which they all find themselves. It is the moment of self-revelation. In torturing
both the impractical idealist and the naïve realist, she
is also punishing herself for her impatience with them.
She too is impotent, after all. Jack's arrival with Bessie
simply brings the paradox into prominence; Nurse
forces her lover to turn into her enemy and pushes
Orderly into confessing what he really is—"his back to
the wall." The mood of this scene recalls the earlier

moment in the play, where Nurse appears victimized and Father assumes the role of implacable judge. In the last scene of the play, Nurse becomes her own judge and victim. In her self-awareness and self-condemnation she carries the burden of the tragic dilemma. No one else proves worthy of the challenge.

The structure of the play actually leaves very little room for social drama. The focus, after the first scene, is on Nurse and her gradual recognition of conflicting purposes in herself and in others. The reappearance of Jack at the end completes the psychological explication by way of contrast and highlights the collapse of Nurse. The seeming inconsistencies in her character, the unreconciled and unacknowledged impulses which move her to action, her sense of impotence are the core of the play. In spite of the negative role in which she is cast, and perhaps in spite of Albee's somewhat confused dramatic purpose, she emerges as the "heroic" figure of the play, made helpless not by the social values to which she adheres, but by her own consciousness of "the disparity between things as they are, and as they should be," of the hopelessness of either admitting the truth or lying about it. Her tragic predicament is beautifully summed up in her ironic "I am tired of my skin. . . ." In the harsh outlines of the social theme, the subtle fluctuations of her character can easily be minimized, especially since there is little that can really be called attractive about her. To overlook the dilemma she embodies, however, is to miss the most significant and successful feature of this early play.

Nurse is the embodiment of the existential paradox. Her will is strong, but with every assertion she becomes more empty, more despairing. The last scene represents the climax of her insight into frustration; her fury toward Intern and Orderly is the final willful expression of impotence. In *The Sandbox* and *The American*

Dream, the double role of agent and victim is separated; it is Grandma in both these plays who appears as the enlightened critic, and Mommy who in her cruelty and stupidity acts as a foil. The two plays should be discussed together because, even if we had not been assured by the author that the shorter piece was *extracted* from *The American Dream* (begun before *The Sandbox,* but finished later), it is obvious that the characters are from the same psychological mold and the situation of the one play is nothing but an extension of the problem described in the other.

In these plays, as in *The Death of Bessie Smith,* the social theme is the initial dramatic premise. What Albee wrote in the preface to *The American Dream* applies just as well to *The Sandbox*: both plays are, on the surface at least, "an examination of the American scene, an attack on the substitution of artificial for real values in our society, a condemnation of complacency, cruelty, emasculation and vacuity; it is a stand against the fiction that everything in this slipping land of ours is peachy-keen." But Albee himself suggests a broader canvas, "a picture of our time" which transcends the personal and the private to expose "the anguish of us all."

The larger meaning is suggested, in the context of the play, by a tendency—developed and finally perfected in the full-length plays—to strip away the *accidents* of personality and show its *substance* (or lack of it). The characters in *The Sandbox* and *The American Dream* are Everyman and the Temptations he must face (and the Rewards he wins): The Young Man (in the shorter play, The Angel of Death), Mommy, Daddy, Grandma. These characters are closer to types, and the situation they define is reminiscent of allegories. Instead of depicting the conflict of personality—the inner contradictions of intention and action—Albee here externalizes

human motivation and reduces it to a vivid clash of
wills. The technique has many of the weaknesses of a
genial plan sketched out for the first time; behind it,
however, is the confidence of the artist who knows a
good thing when he sees it. This attempt at stark pro-
files is interesting also as the first indication of Albee's
mature style. In moving toward abstraction of this kind,
the dramatist is in fact abandoning social themes; and
in emptying out character, he is also stripping dramatic
action to its essentials. To grasp quickly the value of
this early experimentation, one need only mention *Tiny
Alice*, where allegory becomes an immediate fact and
the strange people who sustain it—like the inhabitants
of some Dantesque hell—are stripped down to their
characteristic "act," their peculiar individuality intensi-
fied by virtue of the reduction.

The Sandbox and *The American Dream* are grotesque
in the true manner of the absurd. Humor, as in so
many passages of *The Divine Comedy*, rises out of a
painful juxtaposition of pathos and meanness. The
sandbox in which Grandma is laid to rest may suggest
the sad, childlike quality of senility (what the Italians
sum up in the single word *rimbambito*), but the effect
is one of acute discomfort, embarrassment, exaggeration
—the same contradictory feelings one experiences watching the homosexual teacher of Dante, Brunetto Latini,
scamper like mad to rejoin his companions, after having talked nostalgically with Dante about how *men become gods through thought*. The sandbox doesn't make
us smile, though it is funny; and Grandma's barbs, like
so much old-time vaudeville humor, make us wince.
Like the canto alluded to, the whole play is a grotesque
parody. Grandma herself doesn't seem to mind the
sandbox too much, once she settles down in it, and she
actually enjoys it after a while, covering herself with
sand the way a child might do in one of the playpens

along New York's Riverside Drive, under the watchful eye of Mother. Mommy, in fact, is right there with Daddy beside her, while the horrible masque takes place; and when the rumble in the distance announces that the "time has come," she utters the clichés which cover up the inadequacies of such moments and hurries away. In another context, her insensitivity and the commonplaces she resorts to might produce a smile; but here the best we can do is grimace at her description of the place of death as "warm as toast," at her obvious enjoyment of her role of bereaved, at the tears she sheds as the music—like the music piped in at funeral parlors —softens her indifference into self-pity, at her bright efficiency—"Well! Our long night is over. We must put away our tears, take off our mourning . . . and face the future. It's our duty." She can't wait to get away. And Grandma, in the same grotesque vein, "plays dead" to be rid of her.

The symbolism (the sandbox is the perfect example) has a shifting quality which frustrates any attempt at precise equivalents. It grows in meaning even as we watch. The sandbox is the grave, regression, dreams, heaven, escape, peace, even sexual fulfillment. The Young Man is the male body beautiful, eternal youth, generosity, love, what is gone, what is to come, sympathy, understanding, compassion. His caress brings gentle release, for listening to him and watching him, Grandma forgets everything else. She is completely taken with him; she addresses him as "honey," "sweetie," "dear," and welcomes his attentions. Her bitterness and irritability fade as she turns to him; he makes her forget the "big cow" who sits nearby looking properly grief-stricken. His beauty is attractive all by itself; but he also has the rare quality of outgoing love. Under his friendly gaze, Grandma relaxes; his little bit of rhetoric actually amuses her. There is nothing false in him, nothing to be feared. His very embarrassment at the speech as to why he has come, reassures her that he can be trusted. She compliments him on his way of doing things and accepts his kiss gratefully, as a mistress might, lapsing into sleep.

Brief as it is, *The Sandbox* goes far beyond the obvious criticism of American life. Social commentary is translated into a larger equation, as in *The Death of Bessie Smith*, but—as in the earlier play—the dramatic idiom and the types are peculiarly American.

What is uniquely and most unmistakably American is the matriarchal complex which reduces the head of the family to unmanly impotence. This theme is expanded in *The American Dream*, where it becomes a merciless harangue against female domination—Daddy whines and Mommy dismisses him with a little laugh; Daddy is vague, Mommy horribly efficient; Mommy asks for Daddy's opinion, but he knows better than to contradict her. In *The American Dream* this perverse reversal of authority is painfully spelled out. Mommy not only decides everything but insists on the approval of others. Her fuss over the wheat-colored hat is a perfect example of self-indulgence in triviality. She admits that the hat she returned and the hat she was given in exchange for it are one and the same; what matters is getting satisfaction in being heard, in being told she was right, in being catered to, although everyone involved—including Mommy herself—knows it's all an act. In the void which is her life, Mommy gets satisfaction by insisting on her way. She exists simply to exert her will on others. Even when there is logic in her mania (which is rare), it is difficult to overlook the sadistic pleasure she derives from being in control.

The play is close in mood to *The Death of Bessie Smith*: there is the same pathological obsession with authority, the same hysterical quality, the same threatening feeling, as if we were straining on the edge of a precipice trying to get a foothold. In the disposition of characters, and particularly in the polarity embodied in Mommy and Grandma, however, the play is the natural dramatic extension of *The Sandbox*. The motifs of the shorter piece are here enriched and sharpened into unbearable juxtaposition. The play has also a striking new feature: for the first time, Albee tries his hand at the idiom of the absurd in a total situation which is a whole series of familiar, everyday confrontations. The allegory is not static but moving; there is a cumulative progression from nonsense to logic, from depth to surface motivation, from statement to ironic implication. The play is not really a criticism of the American family or even of the American scene, but an incisive comment on the lie in us all. In a sense, it is not criticism at all; the uncompromising invective of *The Sandbox* here takes on a Pirandellian quality in its search for metaphysical meaning. In the true absurd tradition, that meaning keeps eluding us—unless it is hidden in one of Grandma's boxes. It is constantly suggested in the figure of the Young Man, who is perhaps the closest approximation to what may be called the ultimate statement of reality: meaning, like the Young Man, is a stunted growth, a contradictory *fact*, a reminder of uncertainty, depravation, questions, not unlike Signora Ponza in Pirandello's *Right You Are!*

Mommy and Daddy are shown in their eternal wait for the Image, certainty, the Dream in us all. Mrs. Barker and the Young Man are approximations of the Image. Both of them appear in answer to Mommy's willful persistence and Daddy's acquiescence. The will is strong and in true Pirandellian guise creates something in its own perverse likeness; the inertia which follows in the path of that will accepts the likeness. Mrs. Barker is Mommy in her public role; the Young

Man is the stunted will made flesh. As in Pirandello's play, reality turns out to be what we create—or half create—and where the soul is weak or maimed, the creature it produces will be of the same kind.

Mrs. Barker and Mommy resemble one another even to the expressions they use. Mrs. Barker will judge Mommy's house in almost the exact words Mommy uses to describe her chairwoman friend—"a dreadful woman, you don't know her; she has dreadful taste, two dreadful children, a dreadful house, and an absolutely adorable husband who sits in a wheel chair all the time. . . . She's just a dreadful woman, but she IS chairman of our woman's club, so naturally I'm terribly fond of her." Mrs. Barker will prove she lives in the same universe, in judging Mommy's house.

Daddy listens impassively to Mommy's authoritative conclusions, trying in his own way to become an adorable husband. He has almost succeeded, in fact; psychologically, he is already in a "wheel chair." Neither he nor the others in the household can stand up to her effectively. Grandma, the most outspoken in the house, cannot in her uselessness and age do anything to change the situation; her biting criticism serves an important purpose nonetheless.

Grandma is the Prospero of the piece, who gives a semblance of meaning and purpose to the others. It is she who reveals to Mrs. Barker why she has been called; and it is she also who instructs the Young Man as to his new role. The solution she suggests and shapes is not entirely satisfactory, but without her there would have been no solution at all. Grandma, like Signor Laudisi in Pirandello's play, is the midwife who brings about the stunted birth willed—in their different ways—by the others. Once her boxes, containing the blind Pekinese, the television set, old letters, "a couple of regrets," and presumably her enema bags, have been carried out, she disappears from the action. That is, she hides in the wings and watches things fall into place, telling us when the play is over. Like a providential, detached agent, she pauses just outside the scene to admire her handiwork. The Young Man, like the Angel of Death in *The Sandbox*, has freed her from the parody of life as defined by Mommy. In *The American Dream* the Young Man is also the redeemer, filling the vacancy left by Grandma and assuming the burden for her, ready to satisfy Mommy and Daddy in their vanity and vices.

The family situation dominated by Mommy is easy enough to recognize; the difficulty lies in the unusual superimposition of meaning on appearance, the shock of contradictions, the often crude revelations of unspoken impulses, especially the quiet obscenity, the stifled violence, the recurring theme of Sex—or, more properly, perverted or repressed Sex—as the mainspring of the action. Mommy has managed to castrate Daddy's masculine superiority as neatly as the "doctors took out something that was there and put in something that wasn't there." Daddy is slowly being cut down to size; Mommy's design has almost been realized. She is horribly direct in accomplishing her purpose, insulting in her self-righteousness. Daddy's money is rightfully hers because "I used to let you get on top of me and bump your uglies." Even this basic assertion of masculinity was destroyed early in the game, when Mommy took to sleeping in Grandma's room "when Daddy got fresh"; and Daddy got the message soon enough because after a while he didn't "want to get fresh . . . any more." That danger too is past. But Mommy isn't taking any chances; she is constantly on the alert, watching for signs of regression, of masculine authority, and nipping them in the bud. She has, in fact, mastered the fine art of telling Daddy what to think, as in the suggestion about putting Grandma away. Her tactics verge on the grotesque when "they" finally arrive to take Grandma to the home—and Daddy threatens to forget his lines. The mask of stifled virility slips off for a moment, but Mommy deftly puts it back again, with cool efficiency.

DADDY   I think we should talk about it some more. Maybe we've been hasty . . . a little hasty, perhaps. [*Doorbell rings again*] I'd like to talk about it some more.

MOMMY   There's no need. You made up your mind; you were firm; you were masculine and decisive.

DADDY   We might consider the pros and the . . .

MOMMY   I won't argue with you; it has to be done; you were right. Open the door.

DADDY   But I'm not sure that . . .

MOMMY   Open the door.

DADDY   Was I firm about it?

MOMMY   Oh, so firm; so firm.

DADDY   And was I decisive?

MOMMY   SO decisive! Oh, I shivered.

DADDY   And masculine? Was I really masculine?

MOMMY   Oh, Daddy, you were so masculine; I shivered and fainted.

There's a hypnotic quality about the exchange, in Daddy trying to salvage his male dignity and Mommy feeding him the lines. The conversation is ridiculous, but in a frightening way. It is not so much Daddy's weakness that disturbs, as Mommy's unswerving intention. She has a devilish knack for saying the "right" thing; her cleverness is awe-inspiring and terrible. She seems to have a natural talent for asserting her will. Her feelings are rooted in undiluted selfishness, but unlike Nurse—who could never temper her violent moods to the necessity of the moment—Mommy has perfect control. She is nothing but a bundle of sheer egoism.

Her perverted sexual instincts are the mainspring of her selfishness. Grandma's account of how Mommy "mutilated" the original baby (the twin of the Young Man)—a masterpiece in the use of clichés made to work on a symbolic level—provides marvelous insight into Mommy's hypocritical denial of sex and Mrs. Barker's own "penchant for pornography." The passage is a striking example of Albee's mature powers at work, particularly in its pace and rhythm, which suggest a kind of slow-motion dance—two steps forward (Grandma's revelations), one back (Mrs. Barker's responses)—and in the cumulative effect of a logical continuity built up through irony. It is the first direct attempt at the manner and style of *Who's Afraid of Virginia Woolf?*—indeed, the myth about the son, in the full-length play, has its origin here. The American Dream becomes, in the later play, the Private Dream of a couple much more interesting and provoking than Mommy and Daddy; and although this later Dream never actually appears, he is as intimately involved in the life of his "parents" as the Young Man is with Mommy and Daddy.

The brutal description of the baby's mutilation, in *The American Dream*, is softened not only by metaphor-clichés and a vaudeville type humor, but also by transparent symbolism. The Young Man is the American Dream come back—or, more precisely, Mommy's Dream; but Mommy, for Albee, represents Destructive Woman, and so the Dream becomes universalized as a monstrous conceit. Mommy's puritanical excesses, her disgust with sex, and her irresistible propensity for lust (she is attracted to the Young Man in this way and "sidles up to him a little") are meant to account for the destruction of the baby and the inability of the Young Man, his twin, to feel any deep emotion. The situation is immediately suggestive; it implies much more than the criticism of American family life or an easy explanation for homosexuality. The play, in fact, raises a pro-

vocative question: if we are merely acted upon—as the
Young Man's account of his condition leads us to conclude—then human freedom is a myth. In a universe
where *action* is reduced to *reaction,* we are nothing more
than exotic vegetables and no one is directly responsible
for anyone else's behavior—or his own. Albee of course is
aware of the existential predicament, but his characters
do not accept it wholeheartedly. In this, the criticism
leveled against him is justified, for those passages where
the protagonists seem to affirm the notion of social responsibility are the least convincing. The answers at
such moments are too pat; they lack the balanced analysis such moments require to convince. Mommy, after
all, is as much a victim as the others in the play. And
the Young Man is not completely innocent. Luckily,
the power of the play lies elsewhere.

As the *Doppelgänger* of the baby who was mutilated
soon after birth, the Young Man reinforces the theme
of incommunicability. The American Dream is the
frustration which results from the disparity between
things as they are and things as they ought to be. He is
the existential question made flesh. In his presence
Grandma changes her tone and mood, as though recognizing an awesome mystery. He is the symbol of the impossibility of human contact—but their encounter suggests some sort of genuine communication. Grandma
responds to him in a profoundly human way, forgetting
her own egotistic impulses long enough to be helpful
to him. The pathos he evokes is genuine enough; but he
cannot ever understand or participate in the experience
of selfless love. In him, symbol and allegory are embodied in an unanswerable question.

The dilemma of the play is reinforced in many ways,
particularly in the dialogue, which is built on sharp contradictions. Mommy's greeting to Mrs. Barker—"Won't
you take off your dress?"—and Mrs. Barker's reply—"I

don't mind if I do"—sets up an inner exchange which is stripped of conventional forms and establishes an ironic identity between Mommy and her guest. They both indulge in a kind of perverted sexual satisfaction which has obviously increased in proportion to their avowed dislike of physical contact. Each recognizes in the other the mask of propriety, the same values, the same vices. When Mrs. Barker turns to Mommy with "My, what an unattractive apartment you have!" a double irony is established: in addition to the obvious contradiction in the phrase itself there is the echo of Mommy's appraisal of the chairwoman's home and family.

All this is clever and witty, but not really funny. Humor, in Albee, becomes a trap; to laugh at any of these things is to laugh at our own expense. We may be amused, for example, at Grandma's boxes, at her attempt to gather together such disparate things as a television set, a blind Pekinese, old letters, "a couple of regrets," her "Sunday teeth," and a "few garbled images," but to laugh at them means to laugh at our own precious scraps of vanity. Grandma's boxes are the emptiness around which we wrap our illusions.

In this type of allegorical conception, the very characters are ironic symbols. They are not, properly speaking, *individuals* but rather states of *mind* or *conscience*, of guilt and sin and apathy and regret and indifference—often in opposition to one another. We seem to be gazing *behind* faces rather than *at* them. Such characterization approximates *types*—but this too needs explaining. The term as used since the time of the *commedia dell'arte* has meant the embodiment of this or that characteristic, an exaggerated portrait, a caricature. But the people in Albee's plays are not so much embodiments of a dominant trait as fluid states, dissolving masks, a series of psychological X-rays. The Young Man, for instance, may suggest a homosexual type, but it would be difficult to point to the dominant trait or the characteristic which he embodies. In a sense, he *is* an abstraction; but his awareness of his own predicament, his tender moments, his instinctive recognition of Grandma as a kindred soul, his role as *Doppelgänger*, his very appearance on the spot at that particular moment in the action—as if called there by some inexorable fate—point to a more complicated and subtle definition of *type*. He says he is one thing and acts as though the very opposite; the double image he embodies is not one thing but the fragmented pieces of a perverted identity.

Whatever their ultimate value in *The American Dream*, Albee's initial experiments with such figures and with the allegorical articulation he provides for them, proved a worthwhile experience for the later plays. In *Who's Afraid of Virginia Woolf?* ironic dialectic is perfected to the point of rejecting even the suggestion of types or allegory, while raising the individual and the particular to large universal terms. In *Tiny Alice*, Albee picks up the challenge of abstracting particulars in a new way, against a setting which is itself a provocative symbol. Against such a background, types or allegorical representations become autonomous; even in their most symbolic poses, they are disarmingly human. In these later characterizations, Albee returns in a way to the realism of his first plays, *The Zoo Story* and *The Death of Bessie Smith*, tracing a new kind of protagonist whose idiosyncrasies and personal features give us the illusion of individuality in the midst of surrealistic settings and mysterious symbolic events. Abstract realism and abstract symbolism come together in the full-length plays (perhaps most perfectly in *Box*) to produce a totally new and exciting dramatic idiom.

The Zoo Story—Albee's first play—has been reserved for last in this discussion of the one-act plays, because it is—within its limited context—the most genial approximation in its style and method to the later plays. Its realism is immediately appealing; there is nothing, on the surface, of the hard symbolism of *The Sandbox* or *The American Dream*. In the directness of its action and the simplicity of its style it is very close to *The Death of Bessie Smith*. The action is smooth and natural, without any visible straining for effect. And yet, the play shocks perhaps more than any other of the short works—not through hard-hitting symbols, but through the constant threat of the *normal* become *pathological*—the precarious balance between sanity and insanity. By the time we reach the end, we are uncomfortably aware of a new dimension in the suggestion of a reversal of the two main roles. The technique is more subtle than that of *The Death of Bessie Smith*, where the two opposing states of efficient normality and hysteria remain unreconciled in the single figure of Nurse. In *The Zoo Story*, what seems to be a simple and transparent contrast, at the beginning, turns into a dilemma at the end, where the terms suddenly are interchanged. It comes, in its deceptive simplicity and in its uncomplicated dramatic structure, very close to *Who's Afraid of Virginia Woolf?* and provides a neat transition into the discussion of the full-length plays.

The action is static, though much happens. It is also immediately satisfying from a dramatic point of view. We can identify with the situation and the characters without any difficulty; and our superficial impressions prove basically correct, although we may not be able to explain them too easily. Of the early plays, it is the only one which points ahead to something like real personality and sets up a dramatic conflict which, on its simplest level, is easy to understand. It is a reduced version of the four-way conflict of *Who's Afraid of Virginia Woolf?*; in both plays, moreover, the confrontation builds on ordinary exchanges, platitudes, clichés, and works up to an unexpected and destructive climax.

The final outcome in both is unpredictable and shock-ing. The element of surprise is perhaps the most im-portant feature of *The Zoo Story*; it will not be used so effectively again until *Who's Afraid of Virginia Woolf?* There is, also, in the two plays, a curious handling of time: in Jerry's story one has the sensation of facing backwards while moving forward, and the impression is justified when the *fact* to which Jerry alludes from the very beginning is accomplished only at the end; in *Who's Afraid of Virginia Woolf?* this technique is per-fected in the handling of the Son-myth, although it is there not so much a reversal of time as an arbitrary ad-justment of it to suit the mood and intentions of the main protagonists. In the fictional son of Martha and George, time becomes a psychological dimension com-pletely divorced from reality.

There is, also, in both plays a deeper and more satis-fying analysis of human motivation. I don't mean that it is always clear or acceptable; but there is a conviction on the part of the main protagonists that they have, in fact, understood their impulses, at least to the extent of being able to distinguish the rules of the game. Nurse never quite reaches this stage; she is aware of her con-tradictory impulses in a vague way and gives vent to her frustration in bursts of anger. In *The Sandbox* and *The American Dream*, the symbolic idiom makes this kind of self-analysis superfluous. In *The Zoo Story*, Jerry—like Martha and George—is painfully concerned with it. The whole play is his attempt to make Peter understand what he has discovered about himself and, by implication, about others. As an example of the iso-lation of the individual and the existential awareness of his predicament, the play has much more in common with *Who's Afraid of Virginia Woolf?* and *Tiny Alice* than with the works already discussed.

The dramatic setting (and here too the similarity with *Who's Afraid of Virginia Woolf?* is worth noting) is a long conversation. Two strangers come together in Central Park; one of them imposes himself on the other and forces him to listen to a weird sort of tale. It cannot really be labeled social commentary, although there are some sharp suggestions along that line; the pathological is too pervasive, the opposition between normal and abnormal too absorbing to leave room for much else. Still, there are traces of social satire; and it is only fair to note that these are integrated into the larger theme much more effectively than the social statements in *The Death of Bessie Smith*.

The opposition—or, more precisely, the dramatic conflict—is a psychological one; but in Peter, who seems to spell *normality*, we have also the embodiment of those values by which our society measures success, and in this framework the context suggests also a social and economic conflict. Jerry, in his disarming lucidity, sees right through the social façade and forces Peter gradually to unmask. He is well off, but strangely dissatisfied; married, with two daughters, but really quite alone; fond of his girls, but disappointed in not having had a son; tolerant of the whims of the women, but only because he doesn't dare object and doesn't have the guts to let the cats get at the parakeets and thus rid himself of what is a nuisance to him. The picture that slowly emerges is seen, as it were, at a great distance, but we seem to hear something of the strident quality of the family scenes in *The Sandbox* and *The American Dream*, in retrospect. The shadow of Domineering Woman is there, but it will not be filled in until *The Death of Bessie Smith*. Daddy's "I do wish I weren't surrounded by women; I'd like some men around here," in *The American Dream*, can almost be heard in Peter's pathetic struggle to maintain his manly dignity as

Jerry touches the sore spot and makes him admit that he can't stand being in the house for long with all the women around. The park bench is his refuge, the symbol of his masculine independence. Jerry has understood all this, and in challenging Peter's right to the bench and gradually pushing him off it, he is forcing him literally and in every other sense off balance.

Peter—the successful executive with the right kind of wife and the right kind of pets and hobbies and habits —moves monotonously on the surface of life, pushed on by a kind of inertia which is mistaken for intention. Jerry destroys the illusion by pushing him into action and forcing him to exert his will consciously and directly. The social implications are thus absorbed into the effort to transform external reality into intimate, meaningful volition. Things are rejected for ideas, and important facts are turned into conscious and deliberate action. What "happened" at the zoo is the recognition of what has happened inside Peter and Jerry as a result of their brief encounter. It is also the "event" which results from that recognition.

Jerry's persistent questioning of Peter and his tireless verbal energy are unmistakable signs of an hysterical state. His precarious condition is underscored by the vivid contrast between what we see and hear and what he tells us about his life and habits. We learn, for example, that in spite of his insistent overtures to get Peter to talk with him, he is not at all communicative. He scarcely knows the other people who live in his rooming house, although his quick eye and ear have obviously caught the essential characteristic of each; "the little ladies" whom he occasionally visits never see him more than once in each case; the landlady with her obscene attentions simply pushes him into deeper withdrawal; his mother deserted him when he was ten, and his father lived on just long enough to bring back her body and follow her into oblivion after one last glorious binge; except for a brief homosexual experience as a boy, he has never had a deep emotional involvement. This self-portrait jars with the picture of the talkative stranger who provides it. The compulsion to talk appears increasingly suspicious. Both the compulsion and the suspicion reach their climax in the story of the dog, the dramatic and psychological turning point of the play.

Jerry's account of the dog's antipathy toward him and of his attempt first to draw it into friendship by feeding it, then—that failing—to poison it, and finally, to reach some kind of mutual understanding mirrors, in the length and intensity of the narrative, his mounting hysteria. The story is a kind of parable; it is, in fact, full of allusions, references, phrases, and cadences from the Bible. The dog itself is Cerberus at the mouth of the underworld and Jerry a kind of Jesus-figure trying to storm the gates of hell, which unlike those in the original story, unfortunately will not give. In his encounter with the dog, Jerry comes to realize the sad truth and recognizes in the experience a kind of ambiguous progress toward insight—"the mixture of sadness and suspicion" cancels out into indifference. The dog returns to his garbage and Jerry to free passage in and out of the house. Or, more precisely, Jerry has "GAINED solitary free passage, if that much further loss can be said to be gain." But the real lesson of the story—as in the parables—is meant to inspire to purposeful action. The clue to this insight comes toward the end of the account, when Jerry sums up the meaning of his "parable" as the realization that "neither kindness nor cruelty by themselves, independent of each other, creates any effect beyond themselves; and . . . that the two combined, together, at the same time, are the teaching emotion." There is nothing sentimental in this; Jerry himself is too self-deprecating to allow himself to become a petty prophet. He is as cruel toward himself as he appears to be toward Peter. The heightened tone of his moment of insight points up, stylistically, the climax of the play, which is the translation of his experience with the dog into terms which Peter will understand.

Peter's reaction is a frustrated, almost tearful confession of his inability to get the point. Jerry is furious at first, but he soon recovers as though divining what must be done. He changes tactics abruptly, joking and tickling Peter and suddenly reminding him of the earlier promise to tell him what happened at the zoo that day. The Biblical overtones of these passages prepare us for the symbolism which now emerges of the zoo as a man-made hell, where people are separated by bars and communication impossible. The zoo is the condition of human existence; Jerry has put this revelation to a preliminary test in the experiment with the dog; he now proceeds to put it to the definitive test in an experiment involving another human being. The zoo is the perfect setting for the brutal confrontation with Peter. Its violence must be unleashed if complacency and selfish withdrawal are to disappear. Salvation—if indeed possible—must be preceded by a destructive crisis, like the death on the Cross. In that crisis, the subconscious and the instinctive must be brought to light and acknowledged, Oedipus-fashion.

Peter must be made to do willingly and spontaneously what Jerry has foreseen as *necessary*: reach out in a meaningful gesture toward another human being. Like the Biblical figure of Peter, he must be made to deny his fellowman, and in the denial betray him, in order to learn to love him. Jerry pushes him toward this inevitable revelation by his seemingly whimsical request for the entire bench. Peter is gradually pushed off, while Jerry taunts him into anger, and lashes out finally, defending himself with a knife provided by Jerry. There is much, in the last moments of the play, to suggest an orgiastic homosexual "rite," but the anagogical reading is even clearer: having brought the "lesson" to an end, Jerry urges Peter to escape, making perfectly clear that he is not angry but grateful for Peter's attempt at "communication." The ironic reversal of this ending takes on a mystical quality (it will be explored in depth, later, in *Tiny Alice*); Peter, like his Biblical namesake, has brought comfort and redemption to his friend, who seals the bargain with his acceptance of death. In stabbing Jerry, Peter has bound himself in a grotesque and permanent relationship—murderer and victim become a single irrevocable *fact*.

Jerry dies in the conviction that the paradox of human communication has been solved through an absolute commitment inspired by fear, but exalted through death. As it applies to him, the paradox *has* been solved; but the final point of the lesson is not quite so optimistic. Peter's betrayal and the knowledge that comes to him do not save him in any true sense, for he is more isolated, more alone then than ever before. His denial of commitment is never revoked—in spite of the fact of his participation in the sacrifice; the play ends with his Judas-like flight. We need not follow him into his darkness to know what his suffering will be like. Whether he gets caught or not is irrelevant in this context; what *is* significant is the heightening of frustration to an insupportable burden which he can never share with anyone. The conclusion of the parable is not salvation but despair. The mood is not unlike that of Sartre's *No Exit*.

Knowledge and ignorance, violence and love, cruelty and sympathy are woven into a beautifully suggestive tapestry in this first attempt of Albee's to capture dramatically the contradictions at the heart of human motivation. An act of will is an unfathomable mystery. In preparing the scene for Peter's assumption of responsibility, Jerry takes on the paradoxical role of providence, urging Peter to the threshold of insight. But it is Peter himself who springs the trap.

In its exposition of the paradox of purposeful action as well as in its subdued but powerful symbolic suggestions, *The Zoo Story* is by far the most perfectly realized of Albee's early plays, a flawless gem. Nowhere else in the early works is the existential vacuum drawn so boldly to resemble powerful affirmation, the pessimistic intention of the author so beautifully realized in the shape of art.

3

Exorcisms
Who's Afraid of Virginia Woolf?

"Truth and illusion, George; you don't know the difference."
"No; but we must carry on as though we did."
Who's Afraid of Virginia Woolf?

Who's Afraid of Virginia Woolf? is in many important respects a "first." In addition to being the first of Albee's full-length plays, it is also the first juxtaposition and integration of realism and abstract symbolism in what will remain the dramatic idiom of all the full-length plays. Albee's experimentation in allegory, metaphorical clichés, grotesque parody, hysterical humor, brilliant wit, literary allusion, religious undercurrents, Freudian reversals, irony on irony, here for the first time appear as an organic whole in a mature and completely satisfying dramatic work. It is, in Albee's repertory, what *Long Day's Journey into Night* is in O'Neill's; the aberrations, the horrors, the mysteries are woven into the fabric of a perfectly normal setting so as to create the illusion of total realism, against which the abnormal and the shocking have even greater impact. In this play, for the first time, the "third voice of poetry" comes through loud and strong with no trace of static. The dramatist seems to have settled back silently, to watch while his characters take over the proceedings, very much like those six notorious characters who pestered Pirandello's dramatic imagination.

In *Who's Afraid of Virginia Woolf?* the existential dilemma is dramatized with full sympathy in its most painful human immediacy. The weak are redeemed in their helplessness, and the vicious are forgiven in their tortured self-awareness. The domineering figure of Woman is no longer the one-sided aberration of *The Sandbox* and *The American Dream*; it is a haunting portrait of agonized loyalty and destructive love. The submissive Male is raised to the point of tragic heroism in his understanding of the woman who would kill the thing she loves. The action itself is beautifully consistent; it makes no excessive demands, but moves along simply and with utter realism to the edge of a mystery.

Martha and George stumble on the scene with aimless talk about a black wig and a Bette Davis movie featuring Joseph Cotten, and then settle down by the liquor cabinet to wait for the party to begin. That party, one soon discovers, is not just Nick and Honey but all of us. The younger couple mirror our own embarrassment and our public selves; Martha and George, our private anguish. The possibilities for identification are infinite; each moment is a step toward recognition.

It is a peculiarity of Albee's and a trademark of his that the protagonists of his plays are at one and the same time distinctly themselves and just as distinctly Everybody Else. In Martha and George, Nick and Honey, this identity is perfected dramatically, so that the play appears—from one point of view—a psychoanalytic "happening" in which the audience is intimately involved. The strength of such a play lies in this immediate and growing identification of the audience with the protagonists on stage; the difficulties of the characters, though rooted in mystery, are simple enough to grasp in their social implications.

As in the earlier plays, Sex is the dynamo behind the action. But in this case, instead of an oversimplified statement about homosexuality and who is responsible for it, or a brief reminder of how private sexual indulgence turns into prurient lust, or an unsympathetic suggestion of how heterosexual demands within a materialistic society corrupt and destroy the individual, we have for the first time an examination of the various phases through which a sexual relationship passes in its normal, or rather, its inevitable development. Like Shaw, who shocked a good many of his contemporaries, and still shocks a good many of his readers today, by insisting that love and sex don't mix easily in marriage, Albee is here reminding us of the deterioration which even the best-matched couple will suffer in their sexual relationship if love is not properly distinguished from it and nurtured apart from it. There is almost an Augustinian conviction in Albee's insistence on what sex in marriage is *not*.

St. Augustine long ago described the paradox when he noted that the outgoing altruism of love is always destroyed in the act of sex, which by its very nature is a selfish and private affair, even when it corresponds with its selfish and private expression in the other person. It was his view—and the view of the Church from earliest times—that, for a marriage to succeed, the concupiscence of sex had gradually to be transformed into the sacrifice of love. The sacrifice becomes embodied in the child born of sex; in the attention and care the child requires, the selfish and very human demands of the parents are turned into selfless giving. In their offspring, the parents really become one; the children's claims give them the opportunity of rising above themselves, of losing themselves lovingly in the desire they have made flesh. Where this transformation does not take place, sex seeks other outlets, searches for excitement, gratifies the normal desire for self-sacrifice in all kinds of perversions. In *Tiny Alice* this theme will be beautifully elaborated in

Brother Julian's despairing search for martyrdom—which turns out to be an erotic indulgence. In *Who's Afraid of Virginia Woolf?* the theme is examined within the context of a marriage grown stale.

Albee is no Augustinian, and he might even reject Shaw; but what he succeeds in doing is giving their view added authority. He has depicted in this play the excruciating agony of love as it struggles to preserve the fiction of its purity through a mass of obscenities and the parody of sex. The Son-myth is the embodiment of that fiction. It is the frustration around which the action of the play revolves.

Albee plays on the theme a number of ways, one of which is the introduction of a kind of Shakespearean subplot, in the story of the second couple. Honey and Nick have some kind of sex together, but little love and no children. Honey confesses, late in her drunken stupor, that she doesn't want children. Her fear of pregnancy is also a fear of sex, basically, and throws new light on the story of her courtship and marriage. The hysterical pregnancy which "puffed her up" and made Nick marry her has its own complicated explanation, no doubt; but at the time it took place, it served—in part at least—as a guard against sexual abandonment and a way back into conventional and acceptable relationships. Honey's predicament is characteristic of Albee's handling of complicated human motivation. He neither blames nor prescribes a moral "cure." His dramatic instincts keep him from easy labels; not once does he betray his characters into clinical diagnoses of the kind that O'Neill was prone to. Honey is anything but a case history; in her own way she is pathetically attractive and appealing. There is a kind of strength in her not wanting to keep up with the others. Her childlike trust looks ridiculous in that company, but it is incongruous in the same way that the impossible purity of Martha's fictional son is incongruous. When she returns from the "euphemism," after George's vicious Get the Guests, she says simply, "I don't remember anything, and you don't remember anything either." Her despair, though different from Martha's, is just as intense and real to her. Like the fictional son of her hosts, her innocence is already compromised. The *Walpurgisnacht* is her initiation party. Her childish decision not to remember unpleasant things has to be put to the test.

Honey, like Martha, is childless; but the parallel is propped up by contrast. Martha wanted children and hasn't any; Honey doesn't want them and manages to keep from having them—or, rather, she doesn't want to go through the pains of childbirth. At the end she confesses pathetically that she fears the physical labor connected with childbirth and reveals a very different kind of impulse. The two stories move toward the same psychological vacuum. The hysterical pregnancy and the fictional son are conceived in different ways, but they are essentially the same kind of birth. Both are the result of impotence, or rather, of a willful assertion which proves abortive. George fails to measure up to Martha's ambitions for him as the son-in-law of the college president; Nick fails to measure up to Honey's romantic dream. Both women give birth to an unsubstantial hope.

Sex is the name of the game; but around Martha— the embodiment of Mother Earth—everything sexual seems to collapse. Men are all flops, and she herself a fool to be tempted by them:

> I disgust me. I pass my life in crummy, totally pointless infidelities . . . WOULD-be infidelities. Hump the Hostess? That's a laugh. A bunch of boozed-up . . . impotent lunk-heads. Martha makes goo-goo eyes, and the lunk-heads grin, and roll their beautiful, beautiful eyes back, and grin some more, and Martha licks her chops, and the

lunk-heads slap over to the bar and pick up a little courage . . . so, FINALLY, they get their courage up . . .
but that's all baby! Oh my, there is sometimes some very
nice potential, but, oh my! My, my, my. . . .

In spite of appearances and what she says in her verbal
skirmishes, George is the only man who has ever satisfied
her sexually. Even the suggestion of physical impotence
is canceled out in the end, when George proves that the
ultimate power of life and death lies with him.

The parallel between the two couples is strengthened
by other contrasts. Nick and Honey are just starting out
and have something of the hopes and energies that
George and Martha had when they first came together;
but where George failed, Nick might well succeed. He
is willful in a petty way, knows exactly what he wants,
and is callous enough to reach out and grab it. His plans
are clear and realizable. He is much more practical and
less idealistic than George, but lacks George's potential
to adjust to what the world calls failure. George's
failure is incomprehensible to Nick: would anyone, in
his right mind, turn down a high administrative post
simply to indulge a passion to write the great American
novel? The irony is that Nick wants what George had
in his grasp and turned down. In this context, Nick's
designs seem downright petty, while George's worldly
failure takes on heroic colors. For George, money means
compromise; for Nick, it is the one sure sign of success.
His decision to assume the "responsibilities" of marriage
was in large measure determined by the fact that Honey
was rich; but already he has failed in his role, unable to
share his wife's fears and hopes. He is absolutely callous
to her emotional needs, bent on humoring her in order
to get what he wants. His relationship with Honey is an
excellent barometer of his relationship with the rest of
the world. He will very likely get everything he wants;
but the world will hold his success against him, for his

ambition is utterly transparent. George and Martha have understood this and are contemptuous of him; Honey suspects it but cannot bring herself to face the truth.

These ironic oscillations produce something resembling the oppressive emptiness of the plays of Beckett and Sartre. The inescapable dialectic builds up to the recognition, on the part of each of the protagonists, of what he is not and cannot ever be. Each absorbs as much as he is capable of taking in; the rest of the lesson is there to be heard and carried away in the memory. In their hell, the will continues to assert itself in impotent frustration. The exorcism which finally comes about is a vacuum—stylistically, the play reflects the collapse of the will in a quick staccato of monosyllables which brings the action to its close. The exhaustion of pretense is caught neatly in the tired jingle which earlier in the evening, at Daddy's party, brought down the house. Nothing happens in the play, but reality is changed completely in the gradual discovery and recognition of what is inside us all. Whatever else Martha will hit on to substitute for Junior, it can never be confused again with the real condition of her life. This is not necessarily an advantage; confession craves absolution, but all Martha can hope for (and George) is compassion.

The existential mood is caught by means of ambiguous explanations, unfinished or incomplete stories, emotional climaxes suddenly deflated into absurdity. The scene where George "shoots" Martha is a striking example of the explosion of emotional tension into frivolity. Martha is playing up to Nick, as George watches; when she brings up the story about the boxing match in which she managed to stun George, he leaves the room. Martha goes right on—it's all part of their repertory—and George eventually returns with a shotgun which he raises, aims . . . and shoots. But what bursts out, without a bang, is a Chinese parasol. The tension breaks; there is a moment of hysterical relief—but it is only the prelude to a new emotional buildup.

The parasol is perhaps the neatest symbol of George's impotence in his destructive relationship with Martha. It is given sexual overtones by Martha's exchange with Nick, a few moments later—"You don't need any props, do you baby?" "Unh-unh." "I'll bet not. No fake Jap gun for you, eh?" Nick too will turn out to be another "pointless infidelity," and will be relegated to the humiliating role of "houseboy" at the end. No one can match George, but George cannot altogether satisfy her shifting moods. He understands them and adjusts to them—but at his best he must appear weak. He is her scapegoat, the articulate challenger who keeps Martha on her toes, the constant reminder of her own inadequacies. Martha needs victims, and she can pick them up anywhere; but George is the only one who rises to the occasion each time she lashes out. There is some secret understanding between them; she has ruined him with her excessive demands and her domineering ways; but he has not been crushed. His strength reassures her, even when she forces it against herself. George is her conscience and her accuser. In her soliloquy she admits that all the things he says are true—even to Daddy's red eyes —but she fights him for having said them. In some strange way, their fighting is their only means of real communication. George's obstinacy is the reassurance that he has understood the script and can play it out. Martha accuses him of wanting the flagellation she inflicts, but the statement is only partly true. He wants it because he knows she needs it as an excuse. She herself can't say this, but there is every reason to believe that she has grasped and accepted that conclusion. She comes close to confessing it in the soliloquy.

> I cry all the time too, Daddy. I cry all the time; but deep inside, so no one can see me. I cry all the time. And Geor-

gie cries all the time, too. We both cry all the time, and
then, what we do, we cry, and we take our tears, and we
put 'em in the ice box, in the goddam ice trays . . . until they're all frozen . . . and then . . . we put them . . .
in our . . . drinks.

In this summing up of the vicious cycle which is the
aimless habit of their life, Martha turns a commonplace
into a poetic image. The futility of all that frustrated
energy is beautifully captured in those ice cubes which
will go into furnishing new energy for new recriminations and fresh tears.

In his verbal agility and his instinctive grasp of
things, George has a Hamlet-like appeal. Somewhere in
his soul, his aimless puns have meaning. His verbal
fencing with Nick on at least two occasions succeeds in
humiliating the younger man, who thinks he *knows*. But
knowing means being married to Martha and being
able to fence in that way. *Knowing* means weaving in
and out of irrelevancies and coming back each time to
the sore spot; it means indulging in confusion which is
not altogether accidental. Even his absentmindedness
seems to have a purpose. With a kind of fixation, George
keeps coming around to the subject of the History
Department and his own abortive role in it. His failure
is a challenge hurled at his potential rival. Nick may be
more likely to succeed, but he cannot hold his own in
the hard-hitting duel of words.

The only worthy challenger is Martha. Both have an
uncanny gift for turning obvious disadvantage into
victory through wit, ad-libbing where the familiar script
seems to repeat itself monotonously and turning the unexpected into an integral part of the dialogue. The game
is brilliant and vicious when they indulge in it together;
it takes on a sad, pathetic quality when one or the other
indulges in it with Nick or Honey. Honey is, on the
whole, too naïve to be an effective foil, but Nick is just

self-conscious enough to draw blood. And George and Martha are always ready to catch the faintest suggestion of hypocrisy, any hint of weakness that can be turned into a weapon. They enjoy the game as only experts can. If at times others are hurt, it isn't so much that they enjoy inflicting pain but that their nature demands satisfaction. In his insistence on false pragmatic values, in his false dignity, Nick repeatedly invites such cruelty. The verbal parrying is inspired by the recognition of humbug; irony and sarcasm cut into the surface of things and expose the raw nerves of the offender. The urge is the urge to grasp reality.

All this talk serves, paradoxically, to underscore the incommunicability which is the heart of the play. Nick tolerates his wife and uses her—and, presumably, her money—for his own private ends; Honey is too pre-occupied with her own puffed-up fears to realize what is going on and face up to the difficulties in her marriage; George and Martha prefer to indulge in private games and public hostility rather than face their shared loneliness. Occasionally, some attempt is made to reach out—as when George warns Nick about the danger of being overconfident and using people callously to get what he wants. To Nick, George is simply a jealous husband, the impotent male wounded in his vanity.

Frustration is the dramatic impulse of the play. The invitation to Nick and Honey is a frenzied attempt at oblivion through a kind of saturnalia; the verbal skirmishes are frustrated attempts at communication; the history of the two couples is the story of frustrated love; the accusations are frustrated attempts at understanding; a frustrated prayer celebrates the end of the nightmare.

The climax of the play is the high point of frustration, where George's anger presents an immediate threat and —miraculously—is turned instead into the inspiration which gives focus and purpose to the aimless action up to that point. Nick and Martha are in the kitchen; and George, in his lonely despair, throws the book he has been reading across the room, hitting the door chimes which are set off by the impact. Honey returns from the bathroom at this moment and George's frustration is turned full blast on her. He lashes out cruelly, trying to enlighten her about the hard realities she chooses to ignore—

> There are a couple of people in there . . . they are in there, in the kitchen . . . Right there, with the onion skins and the coffee grounds . . . sort of . . . sort of a . . . sort of a dry run for the wave of the future.

Honey's desperate retreat into ignorance infuriates George; he has found her weak spot—"you simpering bitch . . . you don't want CHILDREN?"—and all his accumulated hatred is turned on her. Honey has managed to find a way to avoid pregnancy without Nick's knowing—but Nick is out in the kitchen trying to "hump the hostess" while the host struggles to contain his anger. The moment is explosive. Both Honey and George are aware at that moment of the demonic force which has been let loose and which threatens to destroy them all. It is at this point that Honey, in her childish attempt to distract her enemy, reminds him about the chimes ringing. To George—who must adjust to the change—it is "the sound of bodies" at first; but his feverish imagination is quick to answer the challenge and he shapes the sound into a purposeful plot meant to punish Martha:

> . . . somebody rang . . . it was somebody . . . with . . . I'VE GOT IT! I'VE GOT IT, MARTHA . . . ! Somebody with a message . . . and the message was . . . our son . . . OUR SON! . . . It was a message . . . the bells rang and it was a message, and it was about . . . our son . . . and the message . . . was . . . and the message was . . . our . . . son . . . is . . . DEAD!

With characteristic resiliency, George manages to turn chaos into meaningful reality. Impotence is transformed into creative purpose; the two separate vectors—Honey's desperate demand for reassurance and George's demonic spite—come together at this crucial moment to give new direction to the action. From that moment on, George is in command, a providential agent calling the moves right up to the resolution and fulfillment of his plan.

In resolving to destroy the fiction of the son, George is responding to his own impotent spite; but there is a certain tragic justice in the plan. Martha keeps changing the rules of the game, after all; and although George has gone along up to that point ("learning the games we play as quickly as I can change the rules" as Martha says), she has gone too far, stepping over some invisible line; she has betrayed some tacit agreement. George's plan to punish her is, by her own admission, the fulfillment of her paradoxical impulses: she needs his love but does not deserve it; she hates him for his idealism but acknowledges her weakness in exposing him; in taunting him she is expressing disgust at her own shortcomings; she will not forgive him "for having come to rest; for having seen me and having said: yes; this will do; who has made the hideous, the hurting, the insulting mistake of loving me and must be punished for it." In hatred, as in love, they are indissolubly bound; in punishing Martha, George is also punishing himself. This paradox is the source of their frustration: it gave birth to the Son-myth and will now destroy it.

Martha's fictional son is the child of her will, the symbol of potency and virility, the imaginative embodiment of all the masculine roles idealized and idolized. He is the perfect lover, the perfect son and husband, the successful breadwinner, the creature of all her hopes. George points up the erotic implications of Martha's obsessive interest in the boy:

He's a nice kid, really, in spite of his home life; I mean, most kids'd grow up neurotic, what with Martha here carrying on the way she does: sleeping 'till four in the P.M., climbing all over the poor bastard, trying to break the bathroom door down to wash him in the tub when he's sixteen, dragging strangers into the house at all hours. . . .

Martha herself suggests a very different picture. With nostalgia she recalls all the vivid details of the child's discovery of the world, the cane headboard he wore through with his little hands, the croup tent and the shining kettle hissing in the one single light of the room "that time he was sick," animal crackers, and the bow and arrow he kept under his bed, her beautiful boy walking "evenly between us . . . to protect us all from George's . . . weakness . . . and my . . . necessary greater strength . . . to protect himself . . . and US." Martha's child is perfection and George the "drowning man" who threatened repeatedly to destroy that perfection. Instinctively, we understand that this exchange marks the moment of destruction—Martha's recollections are the examination of conscience that precedes confession and the entire cycle of purification. George —who has always stopped her from bringing up the subject—this time has actually encouraged her to do so. It is part of his plan.

Martha's moment of grace is short-lived. Having named George in her reminiscences, she turns her full attention to describing his negative influence on the child and the boy's shame at the "shabby failure" his father has become over the years. The quarrel resumes with these accusations and recriminations, rising to a pathetic climax with Martha's claim that the child is "the one thing, the one person I have tried to protect, to raise above the mire of this vile, crushing marriage; the one light in all this hopeless . . . DARKness . . . OUR SON." Against her stark accusations, we hear the funeral service for the dead, intoned in Latin by George;

both end at the same moment. There is a brief inter-
ruption by Honey, at this point, and then George's
triumphant announcement that sunny-Jim is dead.

Martha's account almost convinces us, but there is no
sunny-Jim, of course. By the time the exorcism is over
even Nick has seen the light. Martha's furious "YOU
CANNOT DO THAT! YOU CAN'T DECIDE
THAT FOR YOURSELF!" leaves no more room for
doubt. George has killed the myth and Martha finally has
to accept the fact. But the reasoning behind the fact is
a private understanding, a tacit agreement between
George and Martha.

MARTHA [*Great sadness and loss*]   You have no right
. . . you have no right at all. . . .
GEORGE [*Tenderly*]   I have the right, Martha. We
never spoke of it; that's all. I could kill him any
time I wanted to.
MARTHA   But why? Why?
GEORGE   You broke our rule, baby. You mentioned
him . . . you mentioned him to someone else.

The tacit agreement was that the boy remain their
private dream, not to be shared with anyone else, not to
be corrupted by exposure to an unsympathetic world.
Martha's indulgence in confiding to others, her breaking the rules and telling "the bit" about their "son" is
the cue that private communication is breaking down.
George's decision was not so much punishment as
necessity. It had been "an easy birth . . . once it had
been . . . accepted, relaxed into"; presumably it will be
an easy death, once it is accepted in the same way.
Martha must give him up because the myth has taken
over and entered into her public life. Private necessity
has turned into a public joke. George has tried to protect her from this moment; but when the shared myth
turns into a stunted fact, he destroys it. Like an in-

exorable agent of fate, he guides Martha through the long reminiscences and the subsequent "confession." Having been exposed, the myth must be properly laid to rest.

The "death" scene is one of the most suggestive of the play and, in spite of the presence of Nick and Honey, a private conversation between Martha and George. They speak the same language, but never try to explain the contradictions to the others. Nick and Honey will take away what they can absorb; their reaction—like that of the audience—is the measure of their insight. The scene is sober and naturalistic, in keeping with the "tragic" end of the child. The "eulogy" anticipates the straightforward, transparent language of *Tiny Alice* in its sentimental reminiscences, but it is simultaneously an ironic *ritual*.

Albee takes great pains to develop these two distinct voices here, for Martha's "son"—invisible but real—is the most striking paradox of the play. He is the imagination made flesh—or, more precisely, the "word" made flesh, for Martha and George have brought him into the world as talk, as a game between them, in which he arbitrates, comforts, gives strength to his parents. He is clarity, insight, parable. If one were disposed to take on the burden of a polysemous reading, one might trace some interesting religious analogies, such as the "lamb" and the "tree" against which the boy met his death, and the "porcupine" which he tried to avoid, like the crown of thorns in the story of Christ.

One need not labor such analogies, however, to grasp the rich content of the Son-myth. He is Martha's hope, her way of getting psychological relief, her faith that some corner of life remains untouched and pure. Birth came easily, "once it had been accepted"; but his life was not easy, for he bore the burden of his parents' mutual accusations and suffered the agony of their mutual guilt. Innocence and guilt—the divine and human—come together in him. "He walked evenly between us," Martha recalls, "a hand out to each of us for what we could offer by way of support, affection, teaching, even love"; but those same hands held them off, too, "for mutual protection." He ran off periodically, but always returned—just as he was returning that day, the day of his birthday, of his majority. He was expected back; he *did* come back; but in his majority he forced them into a new and unexpected relationship. His death suggests, by way of contrast, a new beginning, a kind of salvation in truth. His sacrifice should be the gift of love.

Such a reading brings to light several hints of a "virgin birth." Martha refers many times to "my" son and George repeatedly tries to correct her; and in one place, at least, she attributes to George a doubt that "deep down in the private-most pit of his gut, he's not completely sure it's his own kid." George's casual remark to Nick that "Martha doesn't have pregnancies at all" strengthens this suggestion: Martha has no pregnancies, but she has nevertheless miraculously given birth.

In this context, the exorcism at the end of the play is the confession which will restore spiritual health. George, the high priest, has already prophesied what must come.

> We all peel labels, sweeties; and when you get through the skin, all three layers, through the muscle, slosh aside the organs (An aside to NICK) them which is still sloshable—(Back to HONEY) and get down to the bone . . . you know what you do then? . . . When you get down to bone, you haven't got all the way, yet. There's something inside the bone . . . the marrow . . . and that's what you gotta get at . . . The marrow.

In his role of prophetic high priest, George hears Martha's "confession," blessing it with his reading of the service for the dead. And like the priest, who in the sacrifice of the Mass becomes once again the figure of Christ, and who in the mystery of the transubstantiation turns ordinary bread and wine into the body and blood of Christ, George too emerges gradually as celebrant of a mystery.

Whether or not he really is the same person that he describes in his story to Nick—the young boy who ordered "bergin" and who killed his mother and father in two separate tragic accidents within several months of one another—can never be decided with certainty. Nor does the *fact* of such an identity really matter. The story, after all, is George's and the boy in it his creation. Some kind of identity does exist, and Martha herself sets up some curious parallels, reminding her audience that there is "something funny" in George's past, insisting that the story George tells Nick is a true one that "really happened," threatening her husband with "before I'm through with you you'll wish you'd died in that automobile, you bastard." George sets up psychological reverberations of his own in his account of how their "son" died—an account strangely similar to the account in the original story. "He was . . . killed . . . late in the afternoon . . . on a country road, with his learner's permit in his pocket, he swerved to avoid a porcupine, and drove straight into a . . . large tree."

The boy in the "bergin" story and the boy in George's book come into focus in the Son-myth, all of whom are in some way connected with George himself. He is the double image—both father and son—celebrating in his inspired reading of the Latin service his own death and rebirth. The parody of transubstantiation is completed in his claim that he ate the telegram (the only proof of the story he is telling), just as the priest at the elevation eats the consecrated Host in remembrance of Christ's last supper. What seems a disjointed, purposeless narrative takes on a providential aspect even in the manner in which the idea of sunny-Jim's death first came to him. The chimes had rung—as they do to alert the participants of the Mass that the elevation is imminent—and had inspired him. Grace—insight—takes the form of a mystical revelation, a flash of meaning in which the scattered nonsense of the entire evening suddenly falls into place and assumes a purpose.

The Son-myth, like Brother Julian's fantasies in *Tiny Alice*, turns out to be a private indulgence of faith where there is nothing to believe. It is faith that must try to create from its own wreck the thing it contemplates. George comes to realize that such faith must be accepted all the way, to the point of exposure. The Son-myth has come of age; which means, simply, that it must reveal itself at last for what it is. The agony of the end is as painful as the labor that brought it into being, but there is no salvation to soothe the loss. Martha must suffer through it, for there is no choice left.

> I don't mind your dirty underthings in public . . . Well, I DO mind, but I've reconciled myself to that . . . but you've moved bag and baggage into your own fantasy world now, and you've started playing variations on your own distortions.

Lucidity and purpose are a gain—if that much further loss can be called "gain." The religious undercurrents and the ironic paradox which is the result of sacrifice are indeed strangely reminiscent of *The Zoo Story*.

The exorcism culminates in a kind of religious abandonment. Nick—the scientific skeptic without a trace of sympathy—sees in all this simply the frustration of a childless couple. Honey senses something of the mystery and cries out for some small part of the experience. A kind of religious awe pervades the closing minutes of the play; the coming of dawn is the paradoxical symbol of exhaustion and death. The mystery is a dilemma; revelation a trap. The mystical experience is reduced to a pathetic series of monosyllables.

The existential conclusion is at the same time an assertion. Martha and George find each other in the poverty of their self-hatred. Nick and Honey are properly subdued; but in their tragic awareness of the emptiness they have created, Martha and George are redeemed. The Son-myth, like a mystical death, is resurrected in the agony of love.

4

Through a Looking Glass, Darkly
Tiny Alice

Comio divenni allor gelato e fioco,
nol domandar, lettor, ch'io non lo scrivo,
però ch'ogni parlar sarebbe poco.

Inferno XXXIV

To an audience raised on the high-calorie diet of hit musicals and the high-sounding platitudes of our social drama, *Tiny Alice* must seem a frustrating experiment in theater. Even sympathetic critics have inadvertantly added to the confusion by isolating the "shock" value of the play. One writer has summed up the novelty of the experience as some kind of perverted spectacular, an Elizabethan-type tragedy, which is a theatrical wonder but full of sinister implications and blasphemy, a kind of black mass—evil and cynical, staggering in its depravity. Richard Watts, Jr. perhaps came closest to the truth when he called Albee an "angel of darkness," for the play pushes to its limits—its shocking but natural limits—the age-old questions of faith and salvation. It is not a "black mass" or "evil" drama, but that midnight turning point in religious awareness where ends and beginnings meet; for the blasphemous repudiation of a Renan and a despair worthy of Christ come together in Brother Julian. Like Alice in the world of wonders, we see familiar things through the distortions of naïve self-deception—only instead of waking up to a solid assurance, we are sucked into a nightmare. The end of *Tiny Alice* is a vision of darkness which, like Dante's vision of Satan, proves to be a double transcendence: words turn out to be hopelessly inadequate for describing it, and the imagination itself threatens to dissolve in its attempt to reconstruct it.

Tiny Alice is the darkest moment of willful despair, and its presumption is the conviction of the absolute truth of the denial. It is not "Hast thou forsaken me?" but the infinitely more wretched "*Why* hast thou forsaken me?" Whatever Albee's own personal involvement, he has here succeeded in describing the traumatic reversal of faith as an existential dialectic, giving the age-old question all the impact of novelty. *Tiny Alice* is the most impressive of Albee's paradoxical affirmations of negation; from the point of view of form and language, it is also the most interesting.

Coming to the play from *Who's Afraid of Virginia Woolf?* one may feel a sense of loss in the skeletal quality of both the dialogue and the action. There is nothing here of the brilliant, almost hysterical exchanges of the earlier play; in comparison, *Tiny Alice* seems—at first glance—to be an extravagant effort at a prosaic lesson, the reduction of the rich multiplicity of human motivation to mere explication—an attempt which for many does not succeed. But the play has its own brand of magic. The prosaic lesson turns out to be a suggestive allegory; and the unadorned text, the resolution of a complicated human equation. The play is, in fact, the most unambiguous and the most emphatic of Albee's "protests."

In keeping with a dramatic premise which is new and different, the play's setting is a distorted image of the world. Everyday events are seen, as it were, from a great distance—the way Dante saw the puny earth from the eighth heaven. Albee's "heaven" is an empty house at once strange and familiar. We have the uneasy feeling that we are looking at things through the wrong end of a telescope. In this kind of perspective, the outlines of human experience are replaced by the variety of contradictory motives which go into it. Nothing really makes sense, but the end result is lucid, somehow.

The allegorical idiom was announced, in varying degrees, in the earlier plays—the Angel of Death, the "parable" of the dog in *The Zoo Story*, the Biblical overtones and the stark abstractions, the deceptive simplicity of dramatic action, the stripping down of character to its essentials, the peculiar juxtaposition of time in at least two of his plays up to this point—but it is here perfected through the rich symbolism of the absurd. In its use of an allegorical frame for existential associations, Albee has produced a work of art more provocative than Beckett's *Waiting for Godot*, more moving than anything of Pinter's, more original in its conception than the best works of Adamov, richer in its implications than anything of Ionesco's.

In *Tiny Alice* everything is reduced to image and symbol, but the result is very different from the cold abstractions of *The Sandbox* and *The American Dream*, where even the theme is expressed in harsh, static lines. The allegory of *Tiny Alice* is a moving and expanding realism built on intuitive associations. There are no arbitrary "keys" to be deciphered and, like all successful allegory, it includes the entire structure of the work—language, setting, props, and characters. The effect is a cumulative one: meaning grows as the mystery expands. Whatever difficulty one may experience at the outset gradually disappears as the ironic idiom forces itself upon us. The allegory is also a lesson in how to read.

This genial handling of form and content measures

the distance covered since the static, fragmented symbolism of *The Sandbox* and *The American Dream*. Seen in
retrospect, the symbolism of the one-act plays may seem
obvious, the characters rigidly circumscribed by their
puppetlike behavior. Still, those first efforts must not
be undermined; modest as they must seem by contrast
with *Tiny Alice*, they were Albee's first conscious exer-
cises in reducing the confusion of reality to symbolic
essentials. In *Tiny Alice* the technique is brought to
perfection. With an ever-shifting symbolism which is
both precise and suggestive, solid and transparent, new
and familiar, Albee controls and shapes his difficult
theme, destroying before our very eyes the world of
common sense and logic. What we have is not stark
allegory but the transformation of the real into the
allegorical. The instruments of this new method—tried
and tested in the earlier plays—here take on a natural
fluency. Allegory is shaped into dramatic intuition rather
than enigmatic meaning. And although the temptation
to find exact correspondences is irresistible, the illusion
of realism is equally demanding. Miss Alice is perfectly
convincing, to the very end, as an eccentric recluse;
Lawyer, true-to-life as a shrewd businessman; Butler,
wholly believable as the caretaker of a huge mansion,
who reflects in his quiet authority the eccentricities of
his mistress; Julian, perfectly real as an inexperienced
cleric; Cardinal, the prototype of the corrupt churchman.

The opening scene establishes at once what will be
the prevailing mood and idiom of the play. The hostility
between Cardinal and Lawyer is, at first glance, the
familiar battle between hypocrisy and righteous indig-
nation. In this context, we side with Lawyer against
Cardinal—as the formula calls for. But Lawyer, in his
fierce, moralizing protestations, betrays a certain weakness and forces us to review his statements from the
Cardinal's point of view. Cardinal may be corrupt and

egotistical, but his superb control, coupled with Lawyer's vitriolic attack, soon raises a doubt in our minds. For one thing, there is clearly a silent bond between the two men—in spite of their differences. Lawyer, the angry skeptic, has kneeled and kissed the ring. His attack is not so much criticism of the Church as personal antagonism. The charges are despicable on both sides, but the quarrel itself is a family quarrel. Subsequent action reinforces all this; and by the end of the play, the two roles have, in fact, been reversed—Lawyer appears, in the last scene, as the calculating oppressor, whereas Cardinal, in spite of his worldly callousness, betrays a sympathetic weakness not evident in the early scenes. In the end, each proves to have been an accomplice in the scheme of the other, and their hostility, the mutual recognition of their complementary roles.

Cardinal's ironic identification of Lawyer with St. Francis warns us not to judge hastily. Lawyer's zeal is not the zeal of the self-sacrificing reformer (St. Francis would have denounced him for tempting Cardinal with the promise of a huge donation), and Cardinal's amused greeting—"St. Francis?"—is a subtle warning to this effect. Lawyer's hysterical efforts to keep Cardinal from uttering the vicious name "hyena" puts him on the defensive and gives Cardinal a certain authority: his words, in fact, draw blood. Lawyer tries to bribe Cardinal by appealing to his obvious weakness; but it is Cardinal who sets the pace and calls the moves—right up to the accusation of homosexuality.

Still, the accusation by itself is not enough to account for Lawyer's fury. His countercharges are of the same kind, after all—and Cardinal makes no effort to deny them. What really bothers Lawyer is the name-calling and the implication that he thrives on the wounded and the dead. We *feel* this, even if we do not understand it completely. It is the first unmistakable key to the meaning of the play. Later, as we see Lawyer stalking Julian—the wounded prey—we realize the truth of Cardinal's accusation in the opening scene. In his relationship with Julian, we understand—dramatically— the horror of Lawyer's perversion, his craving for victims. That he indulges in it as an "agent" of a higher power following orders and a mysterious purpose does not make the reality more palatable; Miss Alice and Butler never betray Lawyer's cold determined purpose. All of this grows on us in the course of the play; but Cardinal's confident charge in the first scene already suggests the subtle inversion of values which is the theme of the play.

Already, in this first scene, there are traces of ambiguity, of hidden intentions, of past secrets; but it is in Brother Julian's fascination with Miss Alice's mansion, in the second scene, that complacent acceptance of reality is seriously threatened. Butler, the efficient caretaker, feeds Julian's amazement at what he sees, especially with regard to the huge model of the house, which takes up an entire wall.

The first exchange between Julian and Butler sets up the discursive method of the entire action. Butler draws forth Julian's curiosity, inviting questions, rephrasing them, correcting them, hinting—even in this early scene—at deeper implications. Julian's curiosity is understandable enough; the model is the most interesting thing in the room. But Butler's manner also begins to draw attention; his confident air of authority raises a doubt in our minds as to his role in the mansion. His conversation with Julian suggests a cat-and-mouse game. Butler forces Julian's attention to the model—the symbol of the paradoxical mystery behind the action—with a calm insistence which is itself a question. Common sense is still a strong and familiar defense at this point, but Butler's joke—"Is there anyone there? Are we there?"—produces an uneasy feeling which grows gradually into a terrifying certainty. When the seemingly harmless question is echoed, later on, it has all the impact of ironic intention. Julian is the measure of our awareness; in him, intuition is gradually translated into fact. The emotional tension of this early scene—Butler's seemingly casual comments and Julian's instinctive restraint—prepares us for the allegorical dialectic on which the play is built.

The mystery of Miss Alice's house and the greater mystery of the giant replica are compressed, at the very outset, in a Sophoclean revelation pregnant with meaning. The suggestion of an infinite series in reverse—a microcosm—is beautifully contained in a visual symbol which expands as the play progresses. The mystery of the replica hangs over our consciousness from the beginning, as the model itself hangs over the room. We sense from the start the hidden life in it; the provocative notion of a never-ending series is compressed in the airtight, Chinese-box arrangement of smaller and smaller replicas . . . down to an infinitesimal question. The house itself is drawn into the question, for it is part of the series. A new dimension is thus created before our eyes; we feel—and Julian's restraint is our cue—that ordinary logic no longer applies and ordinary experience can no longer reassure us. All of this will take a variety of forms in the course of the play, but allegorical reverberations have already been set up with the discovery of the model. In retrospect, Brother Julian's intuition at this moment in the action becomes a premonition. He recognizes in the model the symbol of the confusion in himself; the fascination it exerts is a reminder of his struggle to distinguish hallucination and reality in the days when he had been confined in an asylum. Something in him recoils at the mere sight of the replica, as though his faith and sanity were being threatened again.

He seems painfully aware of a new challenge, a new ordeal. Butler's manner is strange; his questions betray a contempt for logic and order. Julian is understandably cautious. The doubts that have arisen are pushed back, and he goes along with the joke.

In Julian's caution we already sense his weakness and the heart of his tragedy. The mystery in the replica reaches out and eventually claims him; but in his initial recognition of that mystery, a silent bond is established between the unknown forces outside him and the unacknowledged forces within him. The replica is the symbolic core of the play; it is also the symbol of Julian's impossible craving for certainty and faith. As he strips away the dead layers of illusion, the dollhouse slowly comes to life, forcing him to re-evaluate *reality* and the *facts* of his life. The marvelous simplicity of this symbolic representation gives immediate impact, also, to the difficult metaphysical problem which ties the action of the play together. Fire is discovered in the miniature chapel, and everyone rushes to put it out—in the real chapel, upstairs. Lawyer toasts the newlyweds, wishing them well in their grand house, and the lights in the separate rooms of the replica go on, one by one. Julian, in his death-agony, calls upon the Mistress of the replica, and his prayer is answered: the lights in the model go out and Darkness finally spills out into the larger dimension. The allegorical lines traced in this kind of symbolism are tight and economical. The dramatic canvas, thus structured, needs no explaining; meaning is transparent, and the efforts of the dramatist are concentrated in the heightening of the irrational, the intuitive, the emotional. The action of the play is, in fact, a slow unraveling, a Sophoclean awakening through intuitions called forth by fluent, transparent symbols, such as the ones we have mentioned.

As the action unfolds, the house and the replica, or rather, the house which is part of the replica (Lawyer enlarges on the confusion), begins to exert a power of its own, suggesting a giant trap. Miss Alice is the bait and Lawyer the retriever; Butler directs the hunt from a distance. When it is finally over, the house—the replica—comes to life, destroying the last vestige of logic and reality as ordinarily understood. The moment coincides with the wedding celebration following Julian's marriage to Miss Alice—or Alice. It is the moment when the two main lines of the action come together: the chase is over, and Julian formally acknowledges the end of his mission, giving his consent to all that has happened. In his consent, past and future merge; what follows is nothing more than the spelling out of the consequences he has already accepted, potentially. The moment is the emotional and dramatic climax of the play: the resolution looms inevitable as Julian himself becomes aware of his paradoxical role as hero-victim.

His participation in the toast offered by Lawyer—"To their house"—marks his spontaneous entrance into the ritual and his formal acceptance of his role as bride-groom and martyr. At his words, as if at a signal, the lights begin to go on in the model. It is Julian who—without knowing why or how—brings the mystery of the replica to life. (It was Julian who, earlier in the play, had discovered the fire in the chapel.) Now, he is drawn into the magic circle, initiated and ordained into the secrets of self-sacrificing love. The rite, of course, is a parody.

The mystery grows more complex and paradoxically more transparent, from this moment on. The house, we soon realize, is not really Miss Alice's; she is herself a transient acting out a role perfected in an endless series of places, at once new and familiar:

Am I ready to go on with it? To move to the city now before the train trip south? The private car? The house on the ocean, the . . . same mysteries, the evasions, the per-

fect plotting? The removed residence, the Rolls twice
weekly into the shopping strip . . . all of it?

She is not mistress, after all. The house will soon be
empty, and she will be forced to move on to another
mysterious assignment.

The allegorical parallel forces itself upon us. If the
mansion itself has no real mistress, who—if anyone—
resides in the replica? When Miss Alice closes down the
house, what will happen to that replica? The infinite
series works backward as well as forward: the mansion is
the perfect extension of the replica. Whatever we learn
about the one applies, obviously, to the other; Miss Alice
herself can never come out of the infinite series thus
established. She too is trapped.

Albee weaves the allegorical network neatly and
efficiently. It requires no gloss, but at one point he tempts
us with "explication." In the scene where Lawyer and
Butler consider the possibility of telling Cardinal the
"whole story" we are brought to the very brink of
statement:

BUTLER   . . . I suppose you'll have to tell him more.
Tell him the whole thing.

LAWYER   I will like that. It will blanch his goddam
robes . . . turn 'em white.

BUTLER   Nice when you can enjoy your work, isn't it?
Tell him that Julian is leaving him. That Julian
has found what he's after. [*Walks to the model,
indicates it.*] And I suppose you'd better tell him
about . . . this, too.

LAWYER   The wonders of the world?

BUTLER   I think he'd better know . . . about this.

Cardinal is obviously told, for when we see him again
he is strangely suspicious and reserved, choosing his
words carefully, is ill at ease with Julian, and doesn't
show the least surprise when the lights begin to go on in

the replica. The audience never sees the interview alluded to, but the "play-acting" by Lawyer and Butler is quite enough to tell us that our instincts were right all along.

In the last scene of the play, the various allegorical lines which have traced the mystery of the model take on a single purpose as the giant dollhouse is transformed before our eyes into the living, articulate symbol of Julian's empty faith. The festival of light comes to an end as one by one the rooms in the model grow dark, and that Darkness becomes a palpable presence as it moves out of its retreat and enters the larger dimension outside, flowing into the room where Julian is dying, to engulf him.

The model serves to refract and yet to focus sharply our sense of the dramatic design of the play. Julian's instinctive reaction on first seeing it and Butler's desire to show it off introduce us quickly and naturally into the soaring architectural spaces of the play, where verbal paradox piled on paradox, like stone on stone, echo and distort the significance of all that is said and done in the simple turns of the play's action. Viewed in this way, the figures drawn about the model become celebrants of a mystery (Jerry in *The Zoo Story* and George in *Who's Afraid of Virginia Woolf?* had already shown the possibilities of such a role); heard against the architectural perfection around it, the dialogue resounds with infinite suggestivity. It resounds all the more because of the emptiness of the place, and the figures in their show of secret purpose make of their ritual a parody of faith.

Of all the protagonists, Cardinal is the most direct, his motives the easiest to pin down. He is the august representative of a revered body, and his task, like that of a temporal prince, is to insure the well-being of that body. There will always be visionaries like St. Francis to purge

the excesses of the Church—they come into being automatically, as a reaction; Cardinal's mission is the
prosaic one of simply keeping things going. The donation
offered him, like the grants offered large universities
(Miss Alice has, in fact, included these too in her
generous bequest), will not automatically insure spiritual
health (no more than grants to universities insure
knowledge as such)—it will increase the effectiveness of
the working establishment, the physical facilities, the
personnel.

Cardinal is clearly an administrator, not a saint. His
job is the prosperity of the institution. Lawyer suggests
that a good portion of the money will go into Cardinal's
own pockets, but the charge is never proved true, nor is
it particularly relevant. At the very end, Cardinal actually
refuses to accept the money (like Judas, he finds the betrayal of an innocent man too much to bear). Perhaps
it is only a gesture; no doubt someone will be sent for
it later. Still, Cardinal himself is genuinely repelled by
the completed deed and does not touch the briefcase
with the money. He watches horrified as Lawyer shoots
Julian (who will not commit suicide), recognizing and
accepting his own participation in the human sacrifice.
At least, this is the version Albee restored in the printed
text (with "even greater enthusiasm" than that with
which he had agreed to changes in the stage version).
But the bargain has been concluded and the terms
agreed upon; the money will surely be collected sooner
or later.

Lawyer's function does not begin to emerge clearly
until after the first scene, when the illusion of historical
realism begins to break down. Miss Alice's role remains
ambiguous much longer. But Butler, from his very first
appearance on the stage, suggests a providential grasp of
the design of things, in his role as caretaker of the establishment. It is Butler who watches silently over

everything and everyone, taking note of what happens around him, ordering and filing away in his mind what he sees and hears, without getting actively involved in the strange drama. He manages to keep his distance, controlling and directing the people around him with the same efficiency he displays in ordering and maintaining the physical environment. His manner is beautifully indirect. In the first encounter with Julian, he not only encourages him in his curiosity about the model, but also manages to get him to refer to the six forgotten years spent in an asylum, when Julian thought he was going mad. Lawyer had tried to probe that same past, but his arrogance and aggressiveness had forced Julian into silence. In his curiously offhand way, Butler succeeds where Lawyer had failed:

JULIAN   I could not reconcile myself to the chasm between the nature of God and the use to which men put . . . God.

BUTLER [*Almost pitying*]   Six years in the loony bin for semantics?

JULIAN [*Slightly flustered, heat*]   It is not semantics! Men create a false God in their own image, it's easier for them! . . . It is not . . . .

Butler draws from Julian the acknowledgment of the fact. As the play goes on, we realize that this was not a casual exchange. Julian must be made to confess and to live again—in a kind of traumatic psychoanalytic session —his secret past. Under Miss Alice's expert prodding, this initial admission will grow into a full examination of conscience and, finally, a new challenge, a new abandonment.

Butler is never shocked. He is also curiously neutral, even in the midst of family quarrels. It is Butler's unobtrusive appearance at the beginning of the second act that puts an end to the bickering between Lawyer and Miss Alice, his quiet reminder that they cannot indulge in private squabbles in Julian's presence that eases the tension. In his ironic comments, he is both arbiter and judge. There seems to be a tacit agreement among them that his advice carries the authority of force. He never issues commands; a mere suggestion carries the weight of law. His omniscience and authority heighten the mystery of the house and the people in it. Taken literally, Butler's role is strangely incongruous; but in the flashes of secret meaning which light up the suggestive setting, it is natural and fitting. His job is to keep things on an even keel, to care for the house and the people in it so that maximum efficiency may be maintained and some mysterious end effected. He is Butler in name only—or, more precisely, he is Caretaker of a huge enterprise. The mock interview where he imitates Lawyer giving orders to Cardinal comes very close to the truth: he knows all the various parts and acts as prompter more than once.

Butler's unruffled efficiency extends to matters which exceed his obvious chores, and the silent understanding which seems to prevail—that somehow he is in charge—points to a mysterious bond. In their single purpose, Lawyer, Butler, and Miss Alice take on the aspect of an unholy trinity, each separate and distinct as individuals, with personal quirks and idiosyncrasies, yet each—in those very differences—contributing to the personality of the unity they represent. The peculiarities of each actually reinforce the reality of that unity and paradoxically bring them closer. Their common task is made possible precisely because of those differences: each has a well-defined assignment which is wholly and personally his, but which contributes to the success of the joint enterprise. One cannot replace the other. Each is necessary to the others as three separate vectors which will force the action to a single conclusion.

Butler and Miss Alice break down Julian's resistence

through trust and love. Lawyer serves the same purpose
by forcing the action to conform with the pre-established
plan. No one is effective alone; all serve a higher purpose,
an unseen power which transcends and governs their
combined efforts. Alice doesn't exist except as a resultant
of that trinity, the metaphysical approximation of the
single impulse which they all contain and obey: the
final cause (which is both the beginning and the end).

Correlations are tempting, even if not altogether precise. Butler and Lawyer often address one another in
terms of endearment, but they betray no real affection.
They have both enjoyed Miss Alice as a mistress and
come together, as it were, in her—the way Father and
Son come together in the Holy Spirit of love. But Miss
Alice's disgust with Lawyer—her present lover—reduces
the relationship to one of lust, and the unity of the three
to a solid business proposition. The parallel must not
be forced, of course; nor is there any need to do so.
Whatever analogies we choose to trace, they all come
back to one solid fact: the three people in the mansion
are agents of Alice, who remains outside them as catalyst
and final cause.

Butler watches over things; without him the routine
business would be neglected and things would fall
apart. At moments of crises, he is the one in total command, as when Miss Alice—immediately following the
wedding ceremony—refuses to face Julian again. It is
Butler who forces her to finish the job, dragging her back
into the room with one hand and holding on to two
champagne bottles with the other—a marvelous piece
of visual irony. Things must proceed according to plan.
When everything else fails, he must step in, firm but
calm, never raising his voice or issuing ultimatums. At
best, he is courteous and gentle; at worst, ironic.

Lawyer is the liaison between the house and the outside world—the shrewd and vicious member of the
triumvirate, who can deal and threaten and bring other

shrewd and vicious people to terms. Miss Alice is the spirit of love, the deception which traps Julian and draws him to the sacrifice. Her function isolates her from the others in a special way, for the deception must also seem true. She must constantly be reminded, in fact, that she is there to serve and not to be served—to inspire love but not to succumb to it herself. Her feelings toward Julian have constantly to be corrected, her outgoing instincts controlled, her propensity for giving herself wholly, as love demands, checked at every point. Lawyer keeps reminding her of their common mission, threatening her and forcing her in his own way to toe the line. The contest between them takes on a very personal and believable aspect by being described as the suspicions of a jealous lover and the impatience of a bored mistress. One need not insist on these correspondences; the total effect certainly does not depend on them. They rise naturally, however, as we watch Butler, Lawyer, and Miss Alice gradually bring Julian around to their purpose.

Of the three, Lawyer—in his worldly efficiency—is the most callous. In his indifference to others he displays none of the tact we admire in Butler, no trace of Miss Alice's gift for creating illusion. He never really listens to others; he says what he has to say as a fanatic would. The job requires toughness, certainly, and power has made him selfish; but there is something personal in his sadistic indulgence, in his impatience to get things done his way. He is quick to take offense, too easily made angry—in spite of the cold deliberate way in which he stalks his prey. He is omnipotence—power in action —just as Butler is power in knowledge, or omniscience. But Lawyer's job has another side to it that may help to explain the hardening that comes with power. He is not only the *doer*, but the *agent* of revelation, the bringer of truth. In this role, he must be inflexible and indifferent. Nothing must sway him from his task, when the moment comes to break bad news. There is no room for sympathy in this; as the rigorous messenger of fate, his job is simply to get through. Those to whom he brings insight do not always welcome him, but that's to be expected. The negative reaction is familiar to him and no doubt has contributed to making him hard and callous. Like an efficient surgeon, he doesn't see the person, but cuts into the disease. Without him the project would come to a standstill, might never get off the ground.

His task is cruel, his tactics impersonal. He is the most unattractive member of the trio. His cold efficiency has colored all his relationships. Butler's judgment is painfully accurate: "I watch you carefully—you, too—and it's the oddest thing: you're a cruel person, straight through; it's not a cover; you're hard and cold, saved by dedication; just that." He enjoys inflicting cruelty and is at his best in the confrontation with Julian. To him, Miss Alice is simply an object of possessive lust; in his ugly outbursts, he is despicable and a real threat to the smooth-running operation. His egocentric stubbornness can destroy everything. Butler warns him, at one point, "I've noticed you've let your feelings loose lately; too much possessiveness, jealousy." Miss Alice's complaints cut much deeper: Lawyer repels her. He is "degenerate" and his sexual demands suggest perversions. She loathes him with her whole being:

I think it is most the feel of your skin . . . (Hard) that you can't sweat. (He stiffens some) That your body is as impersonal as your . . . self—dry, uncaring, rubbery . . . dead. Ah . . . there . . . that is what I loathe about you most: you're dead. Moving pushing selfish dry dead. (Brief pause) Does that hurt? Does something finally, beautifully hurt? (Self-mocking laughter) Have I finally gotten . . . into you?

Her tone, as well as her words, remind us of the first scene and Cardinal's accusations. Lawyer reeks with the corruption of death. He seeks out his wounded prey with a relish that is above and beyond the call of duty. The name "hyena" suits him well; in this, at least, Cardinal was right.

From another point of view, Lawyer's cruel efficiency is not only understandable but necessary; he compensates for what the others lack. Butler, after all, cannot get too involved in things or he loses his perspective. Miss Alice is too compassionate, too human to be objective.

Of the three, Miss Alice's role is the most difficult. She carries out her assignment dutifully and with a certain wry humor, but there are moments when she identifies herself too closely with her task and threatens to send everything up in smoke. The identification is inevitable, however; the task requires it, although this is not entirely clear at the outset.

She first greets Julian disguised as a deaf, decrepit, eccentric—complete with mask, wig, and canes, to make the joke effective—and enjoys his frustration as he struggles to communicate with her, shouting him down when he raises his voice to make himself understood and complaining that she can't hear him when he lowers it at her request. The scene is comic—Albee himself seems to be indulging in the humor—but the joke is not altogether arbitrary. In the context of the play, it is a brutal premonition of what is in store for Julian. The deaf old hag and the beautiful Miss Alice—like the Siren-witch in Dante's dream, halfway up the mountain of Purgatory—suggest a unity of purpose which is recalled and underscored in the phrenology head with which Julian is left at the very end. The old hag and the wooden head constitute a powerful symbolic frame for the sadistic love story: one marks the initiation into the mystery, the other its resolution. They serve also as visual images of Miss Alice's ultimate unapproachability, abstract representations of an experience which is in itself an illusion. The meaning of Miss Alice's initial disguise takes on poetic force in retrospect, when Julian —left alone to die—turns to the phrenology head, on which Lawyer has in his strange humor placed Miss Alice's wig, and addresses himself to it as though to his bride. The two "masks" are a genial dramatic discovery; they also remind us of Miss Alice's double role.

As Julian's mistress, Miss Alice must be warm and detached, involved and indifferent, sentimental and cynical if the deception is to succeed. As part of the efficient trio, she is naturally aware of the impossibility of stepping out of her role, but her very nature demands it, urging her to abandon herself to love. Her relationship to Julian has all the earmarks of genuine affection. She responds spontaneously to Julian's natural trust in her, his gentleness, his childlike simplicity. The job requires it; but she becomes vulnerable in the process. Lawyer interprets her response in his own crude fashion. He complains to Butler at one point: "She's USING Julian! To humiliate me." And later he warns: "You should watch them. We don't want . . . error." He insults Miss Alice in the coarsest language: "Are you playing it straight, hunh? Or do you like your work a little bit, hunh? Do you enjoy spreading your legs for the clergy? Hunh?" His charges have much truth in them. "She CARES for him," he confides in Butler, and he is perfectly right. It's not the fact of her sleeping with Julian that annoys him, but that she would want to, that she would enjoy it, that she would bring it on spontaneously, before the appointed time (for it *will* happen), that she should indulge herself in her own private emotions while carrying out orders. Everything must be according to the pre-established plan; but Lawyer rightly senses that Miss Alice is tempted. She is prepared to give Julian what she never gave Lawyer—genuine, spontaneous love. His jealousy therefore is real and

justified; there is also fear in him should Miss Alice
take it into her head to do things her way and determine
the sequence of events according to her own wishes.
Their common interest, as well as their common existence, is at stake. In his jealous outburst, Lawyer
brings into relief the psychological enigma that Miss
Alice embodies.

Divine detachment and human sympathy are fused
together in Miss Alice so as to become a single experience. At the climax of the courtship—which is also
the turning point of the play, for it is the moment of
Julian's surrender and consent—the success of the plot
is indistinguishable from the successful conclusion of
her own loving desire to make him hers. In that moment,
she too is transfigured. The success of the task assigned
her is also her own personal triumph. Duty and desire
come together. As she enfolds Julian in her outstretched
arms—an angel with welcoming wings, drawing Julian
to her in the guise of the dovelike spirit of love—she is
both the destroyer and the redeemer. This moment too
—though perfectly natural and spontaneous in the action
of the play—is a symbol, punctuating the third and
central phase in their relationship, the illusion at its
peak. The disguise of impotence, at the beginning, and
the inanimate phrenology head at the end are the anti-
thesis of this image of the life-giving welcoming angel
of love: the three representations isolate and compress
in living symbols the three important phases of Julian's
rise and fall.

In the richness of her psychological attitudes and in
the human confusion which those attitudes reflect, Miss
Alice appears as the weak link in the trinity—Lawyer's
complaints are fully justified from this point of view—
but in their successful resolution to a single purpose, she
emerges ultimately as its demonic strength. Everything
depends on her—not just the plan involving Julian, but

also the psychological well-being of her accomplices. They too are attracted to her, each in his own way. Butler confesses his lingering affection:

> For ages, I look at the sheets, listen to the pillowcases, when they're brought down, sidle into the laundry room. . . . But you pass through everyone, everything . . . touching just briefly, lightly, passing.

Miss Alice is the abstraction of the Earth-Mother Martha claimed to be—desire without consummation, the undeceived victim of her own nature, forever reaching out and forever forced back. To love her is automatically to despair, for she can never really be possessed. But her own knowledge of this is the greatest frustration of all. Butler sums up the feelings of all who have ever been drawn to her; but Miss Alice's despair is even more terrible. Her sadness is the sadness of insight into necessity: impersonal and inexpressible, tragic. What is even worse is that the game must go on forever, that is, until "everything is desert . . . on the chance that IT runs out before WE do." Deception will continue, whether she likes it or not; the same illusions must be fed to have them collapse always into nothing.

As the namesake of Alice, she is no doubt the real center of the establishment, for whom the others prepare and order the stage. Her superior place in the triumvirate is suggested also by the fact that she is the only one who—in spite of the complaints of her colleagues—is allowed to indulge herself in the line of duty. She is the temptress, the spirit of love, the consoler, the virgin bride (the marriage is never actually consummated, since she is acting always as Proxy for the invisible Alice), and in all of these roles, disarmingly human. Her power is shot through with the very weakness on which she thrives. She has often been hurt. "I don't remember his name . . . or his face; merely the hurt

. . . and that continues, the hurt the same, the name and the face changing, but it doesn't matter." Julian's agony is too much for her. She refuses to be witness to it, and when Butler finally drags her into the room where the marriage feast is to be held, she tries to keep from looking at her bridegroom. In the loving identification she has inspired, Julian's pain is also hers and she tries to comfort him, at the very end, until Lawyer reminds her that their time is up. She is her own most pathetic victim.

Paradox and dramatic irony are embodied most beautifully in Julian, of course. He is the most articulate symbol of the transformation of illusion into reality, and reality into deception. The history of his "conversion" is the basic lesson of the play and the chief guide to meaning. In him, goodness and innocence are exposed to a hard, existential critique.

Julian enters Miss Alice's weird household as a casual guest, as the Cardinal's secretary sent ahead to clear up the details of a huge donation. His presence in the house is perfectly legitimate; but we discover soon enough that Lawyer has actually *asked* for Julian and knows everything about his past—down to his father's trade and his six years in the asylum. As the play goes on, a kind of terror sets in, for it becomes clearer and clearer as the action progresses that the people in the mansion are interested in him, not as the Cardinal's representative, not as a "runner" who fetches and carries and follows orders, but for what he *is* in himself and, particularly, for something related to the six years in the asylum, when he temporarily lost his faith. Accident is gradually revealed as intention.

The six years in the asylum contain the seed of Julian's tragic destiny. Like a patient undergoing analysis, he comes to Miss Alice unsuspecting of the true meaning of his experience in the rest home; he appears to expedite the transfer of money, but in reality he has been called to probe into his consciousness for the true meaning of that unhappy interim. He has not been singled out arbitrarily, we soon learn—for Julian has not been altogether truthful about the meaning of the experience.

Faith and sanity are indeed one for Julian; to lie about the one is to lie about the other. A doubt sets in as we witness Lawyer, Butler, and Miss Alice—each in his own way—trying to pump information from him. Is the experience really over, as he claims? The more he tries to explain, the stranger his account becomes. There is, we realize eventually, some dark purpose in the attempts made to get him to talk; he must re-examine the entire episode. This, in effect, is why he has come—unknowing at first, but not entirely unwilling, as subsequent events prove. He has been chosen for a prosaic errand to which he has given his consent; but in some inexplicable way, he has also been singled out for a shattering examination of conscience to which he has unconsciously agreed. The action of the play may be summed up, therefore, as Julian's gradual recognition of this latter purpose and his consent to it. The early part of the play points up the paradox; the later part spells out the slow stages in his consent.

In entering Miss Alice's home, Julian has returned—like some grand tragic figure—to the past buried inside him, committing himself as though by accident to bringing that past to light. The commitment is not and need not be spelled out; it is enough to know that for Julian *faith* is as essential as the air he breathes. In due course, the house—like the asylum—becomes the symbol of his lost faith, the faith he never really had and could never bring himself to deny openly; and the huge model, like the lie to which he has adjusted to preserve his sanity, is the emptiness awaiting him.

From his first appearance in the play, Julian is ill at

ease; he seems to sense an ulterior purpose but cannot define it. Miss Alice's appearance distracts him; she knows how to get him to talk and confide in her. In time, she succeeds in getting him to move in as a permanent guest. Cardinal's business is pushed into the background as Julian and Miss Alice get to know each other better and better. A kind of intimacy develops. With tact and delicacy, Miss Alice succeeds in getting Julian to talk about his experience in the asylum—and at the height of his narrative proposes that they marry. Julian, not without some difficulty, accepts.

With the marriage, Julian commits himself irrevocably to the purpose for which he was singled out. The illusion of free will is thus marvelously set forth. At the very end, moreover, we realize that Lawyer's choice was singularly appropriate. No one is to blame for what happens, but Julian himself. In his honesty and in his own admission that faith is the rock of his existence, he has "provoked" destiny. In spite of his violent objections, Julian is and has been all along on the brink of damnation. His choice of a religious life, like his insistence on faith, is a lie. The lie is buried in the six years spent at the asylum; but in the confrontation with Miss Alice, it finally comes to the surface. The first inkling of this confrontation comes with Julian's renunciation of the religious habit in order to marry Miss Alice. From that moment on, past and present merge in a kind of terrifying Sophoclean illumination.

The six blank years in Julian's life have already shaped his destiny by opening up a question which is in itself presumption and which still lives in his conscience. After those years of suffering, when "faith and sanity" were threatened, Julian had returned to an apparently normal life, but his reticence on the subject is suspect. To discuss the matter means to reopen the wound which never healed, to wonder again about his hallucinations,

to relive his visions, his dreams, all over again and to bring
to its natural conclusion, finally, the skeptical experience
that was cut short before. Julian's tenacious hold on the
secret buried inside him is the core around which the
plotting of the trio takes shape. Miss Alice's expert
prodding disposes Julian to reminisce; but it is Julian
himself who brings about the inevitable collapse. Not
accident but internal volition (not altogether clear,
however) brings about the confession of despair. As in
Greek drama, destiny has set the trap, but it is the hero
himself who springs it.

Miss Alice's interest flatters Julian, although her
questions embarrass him at times. He wants to please
her, grows to admire her, confides in her. As friendship
ripens into intimacy, Julian abandons himself to reminiscences and, finally, tells Miss Alice about his
strangely unemotional experience, while in the asylum,
and his participation in a kind of "virgin" conception—
his only real . . . or imagined . . . sexual involvement.
His account takes on the vividness of an immediate fact
and points ahead to his sexual involvement with Miss
Alice, who will also "plead" with him—as the strange
woman had done in her hallucinations—and whose
role already suggests an allegorical parallel with the
other woman, who thought herself the Virgin Mary.
Miss Alice's interest is not casual or random: Julian's
account of the hallucinatory experience is drawn out of
him as part of the plan. It is aimed, for one thing, at
breaking down his resistance to her as a woman, by
having her share in the story of his sexual life; it anticipates the sexual experience with Miss Alice herself,
which will follow pretty much the same pattern; it suggests that in consenting to the first unusual experience,
Julian has proved himself vulnerable and not only can
be induced to participate in the second, but will un-
doubtedly react in the same way; it confirms the feeling

that Miss Alice's probing is a therapeutic and spiritual
necessity, if Julian is to admit his subconscious desires.
She is the analyst who forces him by slow stages to
reveal himself and to discover the true meaning of the
six years in the asylum.

After her hallucinatory experience, the woman in the
asyulm had announced she was pregnant, but the life in
her—which she associated with her "Fiat" to Julian—
turned out to be cancer, and she died within a month.
Her faith in her own fiction is not unlike Julian's, who
will abandon himself to Miss Alice with the conviction
that in her he has found love and a new faith. He too
will die, having mistaken for life his own destructive
self-deception.

The self-deception is already obvious in his manner
of telling about the encounter. Imperceptibly, past and
present become confused, as he relives the experience,
entranced by his own narrative. We feel the bond
between him and Miss Alice tightening in the fascination he himself betrays in repeating the story. His craving
for love becomes an ecstatic vision of sacrifice and surrender; for him too, love will be the instrument of death,
a strange confirmation of the hallucination still alive in
him. His case is not very different from that of the
woman in the asylum. He too will translate his loving
surrender into a religious sacrifice, an ecstatic vision. His
account of the woman's incredible story is not more
farfetched than his own hallucination to come:

> As I mentioned to you, the woman was given to halluci-
> nations as well, but perhaps I should have said that being
> The Virgin Mary was merely the strongest of her . . .
> delusions; she . . . hallucinated . . . as well as the next
> person, about perfectly mundane matters, too. So it may
> be that now we come to coincidence, or it may not.
> Shortly—several days—after the encounter I have de-
> scribed to you—the encounter which did or did not hap-
> pen—the woman . . . I do not know which word to use

here, either descended or ascended into an ecstasy, the substance of which was that she was with child . . . that she was pregnant with the Son of God.

Julian too will either descend or ascend into an illusion which will enable him to accept the fatal truth already deep inside him.

The purpose behind Julian's reminiscing begins to emerge in Miss Alice's subtle encouragement. At the height of the narrative, she drops her role of attentive listener and interested commentator and takes on the guise of temptress, punctuating Julian's imaginative picture with such seemingly irrelevant statements as "I . . . am a very beautiful woman." . . . "And a very rich one." . . . "And I live here, in all these rooms." For a moment, each seems to be following some private train of thought—Julian not really listening, all intent on his narrative; Miss Alice uttering for the first time, though hesitantly and indirectly, what she really has in mind. Yet, a curious intimacy is established between the two separate thematic voices; each is aware of the obsessive fascination of the other. The same counterpoint is repeated in the later scene, where Julian recalls, with the same fixed concentration, his visions of sacrifice and martyrdom, and Miss Alice interrupts, though at first without getting through to him, tempting him with her proposal of marriage.

This scene, where Miss Alice offers herself to Julian, is orgiastic in its mounting hysteria. Julian confounds his childhood desire for martyrdom with the sexual abandonment described in the earlier story, bringing together for the first time the contradictions in his soul in a kind of delirium. The paradox of sacrifice and sex is recognized at first as a struggle between pride and humility:

Oh, when I was still a child, and read of the Romans, how they used saints as playthings—enraged children gutting their teddy bears, dashing the head of their doll against the bedpost, I could . . . I could entrance myself, and see the gladiator come, his trident fork against my neck, and hear, even hear, as much as feel, the prongs as they entered me; the . . . beast's saliva dripping from the yellow teeth, the slack sides of the mouth, the . . . sweet, warm breath of the lion; great paws on my spread arms . . . even the rough leather of the pads; and to the point of . . . as the great mouth opened, the breath no longer warm but hot, the fangs on my jaw and forehead, positioned . . . IN. And as the fangs sank in, the great tongue on my cheek and eye, the splitting of the bone, and the BLOOD . . . just before the great sound, the coming dark and the silence. I could . . . experience it all. And was . . . engulfed. (A brief laugh, but not breaking the trance) OH, martyrdom. To be that. To be able . . . to be that.

The childhood dream is the presumption to come. The story recalled and events to come define the same orgiastic ecstasy. The erotic language becomes more and more pronounced as Julian goes on; it acts as a cue for Miss Alice, who catches the moment to claim her victory and offers herself to him.

Julian, entranced by his own narrative, reliving his repressed dream for martyrdom (which is also erotic satisfaction), is the perfect subject for Miss Alice's plan. Her proposal is the natural culmination to Julian's desire for oblivion through martyrdom which is also sexual love. The erotic parallels are unmistakable. Her interjected "Marry me" offers a kind of sexual relief to Julian's excited story about his meeting with the woman

on a grassy space by the pool—or this is what I imagined —on the ground, and she was in her . . . a nightdress, a . . . gossamer filmy thing, or perhaps she was not, but there she was, on the ground, on an incline, a slight incline, and when she saw me—or sensed me there—she raised her head, and put her arms . . . (Demonstrates)

. . . out in a . . . supplication, and cried, "Help me, help me . . . help me, oh God, God, help me . . . oh, help, help." This over and over, and with the sounds in her throat between. I . . . I came closer, and the sounds, her sounds, her words, the roaring in my ears, the gossamer, and the silk film, I . . . a ROAR, AN OCEAN! Saliva, perfume, sweat, the taste of blood and rich earth in the mouth, sweet sweaty slipping . . . ejaculation . . . The sound cascading away, the rhythms breaking, everything slowly, limpid, quieter, damper, soft . . . soft, quiet . . . done.

The hysteria subsides but the spell is unbroken; the total effect is not unlike the fascination exerted by Jerry's story of the dog and Tobias's compelling narrative of the cat in *A Delicate Balance.* Here, images of sweat, of abandonment, of violence, set up rich echoes, for they appear significantly even in Julian's more ordinary reminiscences—such as the story of how, as a child, he would go off with his friend, horseback riding, and bring the animals back quite "lathered." The details of the tufts of coarse black hair on the groom's thumbs are curiously like Miss Alice's reminder that Lawyer has ugly short black hair on his shoulder blades and can't sweat. A subtle network of related motifs is thus constructed, forcing upon us the identity between sexual abandonment and religious martyrdom. Miss Alice is aware of the paradox from the start, for she is prescient; Julian will not confess it until he has surrendered to Miss Alice, when marriage becomes the "dark and the silence" of martyrdom. The promise of love is a prelude to death.

It must be noted that Miss Alice does not even once take the initiative in all this. All she does is respond to the obvious. Julian still dreams of sacrifice, of surrender to some wonderful ideal. He justifies his marriage as obedience to his religious superiors, but he is, in fact,

perfectly willing to enter into it. For him it is still
sacrifice, but the memory plays tricks on him. The story
about the Romans and the religious martyrs suddenly
is transformed into the story of the woman in the
asylum, and her sexual abandonment:

> Bathed . . . my groin. And as the thumbs of the gladia-
> tor pressed . . . against . . . my neck, I . . . as the
> lion's belly pressed on my chest, I . . . as the . . . I . . .
> or as the woman sank . . . on the mossy hillock by the
> roses, and the roar is the crunching growl is the moan is
> the sweat-breathing is the . . . .

Miss Alice finishes the phrase, entering into the spell
and becoming herself a participant in Julian's trancelike
state, "sweat-breathing on the mossy hillock and the
white mist in the perfume."

The break in the grammatical structure of the narrative, the confusing of tenses, the hypnotic repetitions
all suggest the intensity of an immediate experience.
Julian responds to his own fiction completely, experienc-
ing the old horror and ecstasy all over again. His impossible dream is there waiting to be grasped: sacrifice
and love, together in a single consummation. The full
implications of his surrender are clear enough in the
vision he has recalled, although he himself will come to
grasp them only later, after the marriage. Miss Alice's
reference to Alice—like the ambiguous utterances in
Greek tragedy—is misleading, but Julian already has in
himself death and desire. The ambiguity is not recognized consciously, but it is accepted in the will. At this
moment, the positive side of the paradox is all he grasps.
The gradual working up to a climax takes on a passionate
rhythm, and his fantasy becomes part of an orgiastic
ritual which culminates in a dying cry as the great wing-
like folds of Miss Alice's gossamer sleeves receive him.

Julian has given his consent; what follows is the

revelation of what is included in that consent. He has seen the whole in a kind of vision which, however, he has not yet translated into the language of familiar reality. From this moment on, everything in the action is charged with a terrible Sophoclean irony: the marriage ceremony and the parody of the celebration which follows are his initiation into his conscious role. In the solemn scene where Lawyer toasts the newlyweds, the secret of the model—and Julian's connection with it—literally comes to light. He accepts his role as a conscious agent of action when he echoes "To this house," and—as a sign of acceptance—the lights in the replica mysteriously go on, one by one. At the end of the ritual, he gives his formal consent with "Amen." Here, as in everything else he has done, Julian is calling the moves, coming closer and closer to the confrontation he has dreamed of all his life. When the ritual is over and the champagne has been drunk, Lawyer turns abruptly to his partners in a completely new mood (which is the old indifference) breaking the formality of the ceremony and reminding us of the true business at hand: the time has come for the trio to leave. Julian, still smiling, asks "Go?" In the ironic framework, the question is purely rhetorical. Instinctively, Julian has begun to fear and doubt; his imagination is alive with suspicion, although the agony of full awareness is still to come. He has married Alice, not Miss Alice. And there has been no deception. He chose to hear what he wanted to hear.

Julian is the heart of the paradox. He enters Miss Alice's household as though by chance, and gradually is drawn into the very center of its life, coming to know himself as a contradiction of love and fear, belief and skepticism, sacrifice and egoism. He craves love, but has indulged only in visions of it; he wants to serve, but he is not clear in himself what it is he must serve or how. His faith is suspect, as the years in the asylum have made clear. In his withdrawal, he has not grasped the perversion implicit in his ideals; it is Miss Alice who will force him to face the truth about himself and make him see that his desire for glory and sanctification is empty and that religious sacrifice is an illusion. His humility is the excuse for pride, his faith is the silence of doubt. The conviction of serving a higher purpose turns out to be a cancer of the will and eventually chokes the life out of him. His ambiguous role is a spirallike movement from extreme to extreme. The truth which finally emerges is the knowledge that extremes must meet and cancel out.

Everything which Julian utters in the final scene of the play points up the ambiguity in his purpose. "THERE IS NOTHING THERE!" he cries in his last agony, struggling for a sign that he will recognize. "I HAVE DONE WITH HALLUCINATION," he insists— and, of course, he has. Even in his objections he is consenting to the sacrifice. The real hallucination was his empty faith. "I HAVE ACCEPTED GOD," he persists, but his God is Alice and Alice is an incomprehensible Nothing. It is this knowledge which slowly takes shape after the others have left him to die. What remains of the past is the phrenology head—the reminder of Miss Alice, of the promise turned into deception, or—perhaps more accurately—of the deception about to be fulfilled. The ecstatic movement toward acceptance is underscored by religious echoes, Biblical citations and allusions. "How long wilt thou forget me, O Lord? Forever?" . . . "How long wilt thou hide thy face from me?" . . . "How long shall my enemy be exalted over me?" Doubt slowly absorbs the old absolutes and his prayers become real questions.

"How will I know thee, O Lord, when I am in thy sight? How will I know thee?" By my FAITH. Ah, I see. By

FAITH? THE FAITH I HAVE SHOWN THEE?
BENT MYSELF? . . . THERE IS NO ONE!

Julian's long soliloquy is a Socratic dialectic, a Hamlet-like questioning of motives which gradually turns into despair, self-recrimination and annihilation of self. In the end, he must confess his error: NO ONE will answer his prayer. God, for him, cannot cease to exist; but He exists as emptiness, the pumping out of all the positive attributes associated with the old belief. The necessity to believe is stronger than ever, but Julian comes to understand at last that his so-called faith was in a God created in his own image—not God the "mover," but the creature of his spiritual needs. That God is rejected in the soliloquy, and Alice—Nothing—is accepted in His place. The transition takes on the appearance of confusion as the two images merge into one: "Oh, Alice, why hast THOU forsaken me?" . . . "Hast thou? Alice? Hast thou forsaken me . . . with all the others?" Resistance disappears as Julian finally distinguishes between Alice and Miss Alice, and his prayers are answered. He turns to the model—"see my chapel, how it . . ." and the light in the tiny chapel goes out. "Alice? . . . God? SOMEONE? Come to Julian as he . . . ebbs," he calls out to the Invisible Presence to whom he has given himself, and the request is graciously granted. He addresses the phrenology model with the insight of his new faith:

> Art thou the true arms, when the warm flesh I touched . . . rested against, was . . . nothing? And SHE . . . was not real? Is thy stare the true look? Unblinking, outward, through, to some horizon? And her eyes . . . warm, accepting, were they . . . not real? Art thou my bride? . . . Ah God! Is that the humor? THE ABSTRACT? . . . REAL? THE REST? . . . FALSE? (To himself, with terrible irony) It is what I have wanted, have insisted on. Have nagged . . . for.

Julian has come full circle. He *knows* now what he merely *said* earlier, when he accepted Alice instead of Miss Alice.

From this moment on, the new faith is uncontested. The "Abstract," the "Real," includes old visions and dreams now properly understood and accepted, the desire for martyrdom, abandonment—everything his soul had "nagged for" in his deceptive sanity. In this terrible moment of recognition, Julian comes to the very threshold of the abstract reality promised him. The soliloquy reaches its climax with his identification of the old illusions with new certainty. "Alice? ALICE? MY GOD, WHY HAS THOU FORSAKEN ME?" Alice has replaced God, and a new creed is called for:

> The bridegroom waits for thee, my Alice . . . is thine. O Lord, my God, I have awaited thee, have served thee, in thy . . . ALICE? . . . ALICE . . . GOD? I accept thee, Alice, for thou art come to me. God, Alice . . . I accept thy will.

Confession and penance are followed by absolution and the gift of grace. In accepting the will of Alice and admitting his previous self-delusion, Julian has completed his examination of conscience and is ready for the consummation of his sacrifice. His faith, the new faith, grants him the vision he has waited for all his life, the vision which he had caught a glimpse of in the asylum. Faith is an empty altar; and the empty model now comes alive to claim him.

The last moments of this remarkable scene are unforgettable for the way in which the difficulty of metaphysical identity is overcome on the stage. Alice is Nothing; faith in her is darkness and silence. In accepting her, Julian has indeed "done with hallucination" and gives up—with his life—his old faith and sanity. Grace comes to him, literally *descends* upon him, as the lights of the model are gradually extinguished by some mysterious hand, and the power that lives there is seen tracing a path of darkness, first in the model itself, then in the room—a tangible, palpable Presence, coming down the stairs, as one by one the great chandeliers in the room also go out. This scene is perhaps the most articulate use of props and stage devices in all the literature of the absurd; mystical meaning and physical reality are fused together in a visible paradox. The life of the Chinese-box spills out, even as we watch, and fills the house—a swath of darkness entering Julian's consciousness and physically enveloping him, just as Miss Alice's radiant white gown had enveloped him in the earlier scene of surrender. Death is the affirmation of love in its agonizing isolation.

In its confusion of light and darkness, intention and real purpose, illusion and faith, the play resembles a Dantesque hell. Miss Alice, like Francesca, draws Julian to her by an impossible dream of romantic love which is gradually stripped of its glamour and turned inside out. The religious theme is beautifully handled in the mystery of an inexorable destiny working itself out through human volition. Partial truths when pieced together reveal paradoxes such as the "anti-trinity" which brings about a perverted ecstatic vision, like that at the end of the *Inferno*. The allusions and citations from the Bible underscore the providential but perverse design embodied in Lawyer, Butler, and Miss Alice. The structure and pace of the play recall Dante's method, moreover, in its allegorical compression and in its swift movement toward a denouement. The play is also and at the same time a series of Sophoclean reversals, charged with irony. In its slow progression toward insight, we are educated in the language of irreconcilable extremes which must be resolved into a single truth.

The symbolism of the play falls naturally and easily

into the ironic design. Nothing is forced, nothing is purely rhetorical. Correlations emerge in the complex allegorical framework as powerful intuitions. Chance, for example, is translated into purposeful action by Julian himself, as he offers a toast to Miss Alice and their marriage:

> To the wonders . . . which may befall a man . . . least where he is looking, least that he would have thought; to the clear plan of that which we call chance, to what we see as accident till our humility returns to us when we are faced with the mysteries. To all that which we really want, until our guile and pride. . . .

He remains true to this principle with that terrible irony which is to be the dominant motif of the last scene. Chance will definitely become design when all his contradictory motives have fallen into place. Lawyer, a few moments later, lets us in on the secret:

> Dear Julian; we all serve, do we not? Each of us in his own priesthood; publicly, some, others . . . within only; but we all do—what's his-name's special trumpet, or clear lonely bell. Predestination, fate, the will of God, accident . . . All swirled up in it, no matter what the name. And being man, we have invented choice, and have, indeed, gone further, and have catalogued the underpinnings of choice. But we do not know. Anything. . . .

With painful accuracy, Lawyer fills in Julian's partial truth, reminding him—and us—of his early emphatic statement that God cannot be *forced* in any way: He MUST be God the "mover, not God the puppet; God the creator, not the God created by man." In his Augustinian conviction that God is Everything and demands complete obedience "even unto contempt of self," Julian's will has already canceled out. His insistence on the omnipotence of God throws light on his later statement that accident and choice are really part of a larger purposeful plan (although man may not see that purpose for a long time). At first, his conviction is Catholic, for he continues to act as if he had a choice after all; but in his renunciation of choice at the end, it becomes Calvinistic and Lutheran. The paradox grows even more provocative if we see, in the willing renunciation of his conscious choice, acquiescence to a higher will. Chance thus becomes design and willful action the instrument for accomplishing what is already preordained and irrevocable. It is the paradox of Christ's last words on the Cross (echoed by Julian), the divine awareness of complete and eternal separation from God.

Insight into this paradox makes Julian's fate a tragic one. The wedding feast was meant to be a feast of dust covers, not the promised resurrection through love. Spiritual exhaustion settles swiftly into darkness and stifles the last vestiges of human will—just as the coming of dawn brings on fear and silence in *Who's Afraid of Virginia Woolf?* and reduces Martha to impotence in the face of her dilemma. But in his tragic acceptance of what must be, Julian—unlike Martha—rises above exigencies and conquers mutability. His death is the freedom that comes with insight into necessity.

Albee translates this difficult theme into paradox and contradiction, compressing these often into a single, powerful image. The language itself, in its brusque movement from cliché to poetic utterance, provides a suitable musical accompaniment to the opposites which often define meaning. At times, such movement suggests ironic counterpoint, or a rich fugue of four or five distinct voices, each following its own melodic strain, and varying also in delivery, pitch, intensity, emphasis, and phrasing. The technique is elaborated in Julian's long soliloquy at the very end—a magnificent tour de force in which the dying man becomes his own ironic commentator as he moves from impotent fury to despair to bitter exhaustion, taking on simultaneously the roles of pleader and pathetic victim, high priest and chorus, each emotional leap defined musically in its cadences, its Biblical echoes, its refrains, its rising and falling phrases, its resolutions from tension to tonic.

These musical variations take on liturgical qualities at times, in keeping with the transparent religious theme of the play. Miss Alice's prayer to her namesake, when the men rush out to extinguish the fire in the chapel, contains many lines which echo the intonation and cadences of a divine service. But the prayer is in a minor key— for the litany alternates with vitriolic name-calling and explosive insults against Lawyer, with whom she has just quarreled and who is responsible for the fire. The tension—self-pity and rotelike supplication—finds its tonic finally, in a whimper: "I will hold on." . . . "I will try to hold on." . . . "I will try to hold on!" . . . "Please, please . . . if you DO . . . be generous and gentle with me, or . . . just gentle." Liturgical effects heighten the symbolism of the two important phases of Julian's entrance into the mystery: the celebration of the marriage—when everyone is called upon to participate in and witness the mystical ceremony—and the consummation of the marriage in martyrdom and death. The marriage scene is, in effect, a musical quintet: Lawyer is the main voice, Butler and Miss Alice the minor celebrants or deacons, Cardinal an occasional reader, Julian the spectator as he is drawn into the ritual of confirmation. The effect suggests a sung Mass, but it is also a magnificent musical aria, consciously conceived in a formal combination of recitatifs and melodic theme to underscore the fact that this is the only moment in the play when all five protagonists come together in a single purpose. Their unified commitment is conceived, therefore, as a *musical* resolution which breaks down almost at once, when the toast to the newlyweds is over. Butler and Lawyer resume their casual banter, Julian falls again into fearful questioning, Miss Alice interjects her compassion periodically (the visual image of a *Pietà* adding to the musical and psychological impact of her carefully chosen words), Cardinal lapses into his cautious but somewhat deflated authoritarian manner. During the actual celebration, the language is formal, archaic even, Biblical, carefully phrased in the delivery; afterwards, there is a return to colloquialisms, staccato and fragmented phrasing, ironic detachment, slang, and clichés.

The play invites detailed examination along these lines; but its chief impact lies in the surrealistic telescoping of real and imagined, past and present, apparent and actual, true and false. There is a kaleidoscopic swiftness in the technique; familiar things take on an aura of mystery, and mysteries are turned into everyday realities. Emotions are painted in all the subtle shadings of the linguistic spectrum, from Julian's powerful eroticism to Lawyer's open obscenities, from Cardinal's pompous show of authority and strength to Butler's easy masking of them; from Miss Alice's gentle persuasion with Julian to her violent dismissal of Lawyer. Long passages of stream-of-consciousness and obsessive, trancelike soliloquies are punctured time and again by the commonplace and the trivial. The most curious thing about the play, along these lines, is the manner in which the dialogue shifts from directness of statement to suggestive revelation—the very opposite of Albee's technique in *Who's Afraid of Virginia Woolf?* In *Tiny Alice* the emptying out of faith is the draining of life through words, and Julian becomes most eloquent when he is nearest death. In the earlier play, words disguise the emptiness in George and Martha—who create the illusion of life through brilliant irony—and settle into monosyllables when that illusion fades. The first is the buildup toward rhetoric; the second, the breakdown of rhetoric.

Stylistic differences point up, ultimately, Albee's constant preoccupation with existential themes. Both plays depict the stripping of illusory faith in Pirandellian fashion; both trace, in a strikingly original idiom, the individual's tragic struggle toward identity. Behind the pyrotechnic virtuosity of the earlier play is an allegory about the foolishness of the wise; and behind the paradoxical simplicity of the later play is a parable about the dialectic of faith.

The foolishness of the wise is a madness within for the Georges and Marthas of Albee's world, and fear in the depth of struggling faith is a Medusa's head for the Julians. In A *Delicate Balance*, Albee will try to trace a seemingly placid course between the two.

5

A Vision of Baal
A Delicate Balance, All Over

The entire repertory of dramatic voices and symbolic themes traced up to this point emerges in a *pianissimo* of subtle harmonies in A *Delicate Balance,* the most deceptively conventional of Albee's plays to date.

Its setting recalls the social malaise of *Who's Afraid of Virginia Woolf?*—suburbia at its best, which is to say, at its worst. There is nothing here, however, of the academic and intellectual pretensions which intensify the action of the earlier play; there is no one even remotely resembling Martha and George in their manic-depressive confrontations. The people in A *Delicate Balance,* like those in *All Over,* seem, by contrast, commonplace and stale, mediocre even. They might be Honeys and Nicks who have settled for a less competitive routine of life, which they can sustain by sheer inertia. The cast, in other words, like the furniture of the setting, is more polished, more expensive and tasteful, but also less interesting, at first glance. And, in the action too, the excitement of raw confrontations is missing; things run relatively smoothly; even the one big crisis of the play seems to be in a low key. Throughout there is an insistence upon dignity and restraint as sheer convention; even insults are quietly civilized.

This calm surface is the most beguiling and misleading of Albee's fictions. Things are and remain what they

seem, and yet—Claire's alcoholism and Julia's divorces
are more than a poor attempt to inject nervous excitement into a rather ordinary setting; Agnes's forced wit
and Tobias's pompous propriety are not simply low-
level repartee; the play is only superficially a sarcastic
commentary on the idle rich and the vices born of lei-
sure. As a total experience, it is as impressive as any of
the earlier plays, although it is only fair to note that the
psychopathic sparring of Martha and George, the obsessive concern of Jerry for Peter, the superhuman efforts of Brother Julian to grasp comfort and love are, on
the surface, more satisfying dramatically. Jerry's total
sacrifice, Martha's consuming passion, Julian's terrible
ordeal—though farfetched in terms of ordinary experience—move us immediately; Agnes's fear of madness and Tobias's dread of exposure at having to tell his
friends they can't move in permanently, though *prob-
able* enough, seem to fall short of a soul-shattering crisis.
In this play, dramatic tension is even less compelling
than it is in *All Over,* where the imminent death of the
Husband-Father-Lover-Friend forces the protagonists
together in an artificial unity which—despite its tenuous
nature—is at once believable and acceptable, a familiar
and perfectly reasonable convention.

And yet, in *A Delicate Balance* Albee seems to insist on such a crisis. To top it all, he drags in as catalyst—to force the action to a climax—something called
the Terror, which he is inconsiderate enough to leave an
uncompromising blank. The mystery—one might be
tempted to conclude—is not that grown people like
Edna and Harry could be frightened by an empty word,
but that a mature and experienced dramatist like
Albee should have been satisfied with such a rotten gim-
mick.

Ironically, audiences have usually enjoyed the play as
good entertainment, as a kind of thing Noel Coward

might have done with the same dramatis personae. Its
neat and not-too-demanding dramatic structure is easy
to follow and—except for the one puzzling element already alluded to—raises no unanswerable questions.
Still, Harry and Edna are not extraneous to the action;
their Terror is not a *deus ex machina* as some have suggested. And this *does* raise a puzzling question: could
the author of *Who's Afraid of Virginia Woolf?* and *Tiny
Alice* really have been satisfied with well-worn clichés
about life in the suburbs?

With the possible exception of *All Over*, this play is
perhaps the most consistently "realistic" and uniform of
Albee's works. Except for the Terror which Edna and
Harry insist on, the realistic representation is never seriously threatened. But the exception is, of course, the
central event of the action: either Albee failed as a
dramatist or we must look at it in a different light.

The Terror that animates Edna and Harry never
really succeeds in damaging the illusory calm of the action because it is refused admission into the house. But
that refusal is, in effect, a shattering confrontation, in
which each member of the household is forced to ex-
amine his conscience and to confess his true motives.
Tobias, as head of the family, must choose between self-
sacrifice and self-control; Agnes must exert her will to
direct Tobias in his final choice; Julia and Clare must
recognize their weaknesses for what they are and settle
for comfortable egoism. In its probing of intentions and
its exposure of human limitations, the play is equal to
Albee's other brilliant accomplishments, up to and including *Tiny Alice*. In rejecting the test forced upon
them, the protagonists reject their better selves; grasping,
vicious, and even naïve at the beginning, they all end
up damned.

The Terror, in fact, is not an external event, no surprise. It already exists in Tobias's household in a variety

of guises. Agnes understands immediately what it's all about because she has already experienced it. For her, it is the threat of insanity—a threat which she describes pleasantly as a kind of joke:

> What I find most astonishing—aside from that belief of mine, which never ceases to surprise me by the very fact of its surprising lack of unpleasantness, the belief that I might very easily—as they say—lose my mind one day, not that I suspect I am about to, or am even . . . nearby . . . for I'm not that sort; merely, that it is not beyond . . . happening: some gentle loosening of the moorings sending the balloon adrift—and I think that is the only outweighing thing: adrift; the . . . becoming a stranger in . . . the world, quite . . . uninvolved, for I never see it as violent, only a drifting. . . . But I could never do it— go adrift—for what would become of you? Still, what I find most astonishing, aside, as I said, from that speculation—and I wonder, too, sometimes, if I am the only one of you to admit to it: not that I may go mad, but that each of you wonders if each of *you* might not—

The motif reappears at the end of the play, framing the action as a precarious act of will, a conscious decision to reject the easy way out, the "gentle loosening of the moorings." The Terror for Agnes is not oblivion, but the awareness that it's there, lying in wait for her. It is not "violent"—but like the action of the entire play, the very lack of violence is the measure of its depth. One must be constantly alert to avoid drifting off. For Agnes, the task is all-important, for without her the others would soon destroy themselves.

Madness lurks within the house long before the "terror" is announced. Agnes jokes about it, but it is a real terror. Clare, the nerve-center of the group, teeters on the brink of destruction, unable to tear herself away; Julia, self-centered and immature, keeps a safe distance but feels the pull; Tobias has seen something of the darkness but has deliberately chosen the comparative safety of habit and routine; Agnes has faced it and has decided to keep to level ground, although—as she herself makes perfectly clear—she is all too often sorely tempted to leap into the abyss.

Agnes is the refuge for the others. She is just as vulnerable as they, but her will is strong and refuses to buckle under. She urges Tobias to consider the emotional health of his family in making his decision about Harry and Edna. It is not cruelty but love which prompts her to reject her best friends. In her willful determination to protect her own, she guides Tobias into the same kind of rejection—although she is just as ready to go along with some other decision, should he decide to come out of his lethargy. The outcome is sensible but sad. Friendship, after all, is—or should be—sacred.

The Terror which threatens to destroy Agnes's world —unlike the psychological and religious forces at work in the earlier plays—is left undefined. It is not, however, without content; nor is its uncertain nature the vagueness which invites indiscriminate interpretation by each member of the audience. These two extremes suggest themselves, of course; but Albee has given us a very concrete statement about them, in his insistence that Edna and Harry never be mistaken for or drawn into the center of the action. Their inexpressible Terror must be understood by reflection, *indirectly*. It is held up, in the course of the action, to a number of articulate mirrors which are the tangible fears of the different members of the household. The Terror of Edna and Harry becomes in that spectrum the fears of Julia, the emptiness of Clare, the withdrawal of Tobias, the implicit madness of Agnes, a series of nightmares which never break through the veneer of appearances. In this light, the play becomes a Pirandellian experience, a *happening* on many levels.

The Terror which Edna and Harry drag with them

into their friends' house is all the diversified horrors of
life. Their coming shocks the others into frightening
awareness of the death that lies in each of them. Their
entrance is the occasion for a critical reassessment, on
the part of each of the others, of their vices, their
shortcomings, their lies and egoism. Julia cannot cope
with the challenge; Clare simply reaffirms her prefer-
ence for oblivion through drink; Tobias comes to the
surface of the truth for a moment, only to confess his
inadequacy; Agnes recognizes the challenge but knows
it is not her decision. Madness opens and closes the play
and comes to the very threshold of the dramatic action,
but it never really breaks loose from its moorings. What
havoc it could wreak is barely suggested in the emotional paralysis of Edna and Harry and in the frightening spectacle of Tobias struggling with his conscience.

Terror takes on as many forms as there are personali-
ties to recognize it. Its simplest reflection is in Julia, the
sexless symbol of sex—at once victim and torturer, child
and woman. Julia returns home after each broken marriage (she has reached her fourth) to find strength and
reassurance among her own. The paradox is obvious:
home is a mirage, a long-lost dream, the dead past, and
in choosing to return to it, Julia is merely aggravating
her already serious emotional difficulties. Tobias cannot
help her; in his own way, he loves his child, perhaps
suffers with her, but he cannot overcome his inertia
long enough to reach out to her in a meaningful way.
He steers clear of unpleasantness, incapable of sharing
and perfecting his love through sacrifice. Julia is, in a
sense, a monster he has created. He cannot help her and
never will, just as he cannot help Agnes who, in her
moment of need, was gently but firmly thrust aside.
In her search for love, Julia merely reflects her mother's
own disappointing experience. Agnes understands
Julia's predicament and therefore does not presume to

judge her. All she can do is be there when Julia returns, nurturing the illusion of authority and stability, maintaining some kind of order, the familiar routine which is Julia's only hold on sanity. When she comes home it is to a sterile past, as a wayward child corrupted by her own vices and seeking—in parental authority—a substitute for responsibility. In her own room, she abdicates decisions of her own. She indulges in tantrums and welcomes the firm hand which puts them down. The hand should have been Tobias's, but it is Agnes's. Julia is doomed to a perpetual search for identity, coming to rest periodically in a naïve optimism, symbolized by the familiar room of her adolescence. When that familiar environment is invaded by Edna and Harry, her latent hysteria bursts forth. Julia is the most pathetic, the weakest, the naïvest, of the tribe. She is one extreme of the spectrum.

At the other extreme is Clare, the ancient Sibyl, who spares no one in her flashes of insight—not even herself. Alcoholism fires her imagination and her cruelty (she is a weaker sister of Martha); she is at her best— and worst—when drunk, most contemptuous of the world, wittiest, most ironic and critical. Her utterances have the attraction of oracular prophecy. Truth ravishes her and she, in turn, lashes out with destructive fury at those around her. She probes Tobias's weaknesses, jars him into remembering what he would much rather forget; like the distant gods, she cannot sympathize for long or forgive or identify with anyone else completely. Her ironic detachment—especially with Tobias—is her image of superiority, her pathetic self-confidence. She loves Tobias and wishes—she says—that Agnes were dead, so Tobias could turn to *her*. It's a dream that will never be put to a test, for Clare needs Agnes as much as the others do. Without her sister, Clare's illusion of independence will be completely shattered; she is too far gone to have anything to offer on her own, and Tobias is too distant to accept the gift of anyone's love. Agnes allows her to indulge in the dream, for Clare's terror is the fear of losing her identity. The coming of Edna and Harry threatens her as much as it threatens the rest of the family, but her stoic bravado keeps her from collapsing under the strain. This crisis, like all the others, will also pass. Prosaic routine will take over again, will restore their illusion of meaningful action.

Tobias alone rises to a conscious, decisive confrontation. His story of the cat—like Jerry's narrative of the dog, in *The Zoo Story* and Julian's confession of his experience with the unknown woman of the asylum in *Tiny Alice*—sums up in a single, realistic symbol the central crisis of the play. The story rises out of Tobias's painful awareness of his inability to say or do anything that could settle Julia's problem. His failure with his daughter reminds him of his failure with the cat. He has no words of wisdom to impart, so why try?

> If I saw some point to it, I might—if I saw some reason, chance. If I thought I might . . . break through to her, and say, "Julia . . . ," but then what would I say? "Julia . . ." Then, nothing.

It isn't Julia's peculiar difficulty that he can't solve; every difficulty is painful to him, beyond him. He has shied away from difficulties all his life; his problems are buried deep within him. Julia's demands remind him of his own demands on the cat he once owned and loved —the cat which stopped loving him one day and which, out of sheer spite, he had put to death. But the memory haunts him. How can love stop? Can it be taken away? What does it all mean? How does one regain lost love? And, if it cannot be regained, how does one adjust to the terrible fact?

> One night—I was *fixed* on it now—I had her in the room with me, and on my lap for the . . . what, the fifth time

the same evening, and she lay there, with her back to me, and she wouldn't purr, and I *knew*; I knew she was just waiting till she could get down, and I said, "Damn you, you like me; God damn it, you stop this! I haven't *done* anything to you." And I shook her; I had my hands around her shoulders, and I shook her . . . and she bit me; hard; and she hissed at me. And so I hit her. With my open hand, I hit her, smack, right across the head. I . . . I *hated* her!

The story of the cat, like the story of the dog in *The Zoo Story*, is the emotional turning point of the play. Much has been said about Albee's admirable storytelling technique, but what needs to be stressed further is the fact that the stories are always an integral part of the action. They are always the key to meaning, significantly placed to provide the greatest dramatic tension. It is Julia's predicament, in this case, which draws the story of the cat from Tobias—just as the story of the landlady's dog, in *The Zoo Story*, rises out of Jerry's efforts to "reach" Peter. The story of the cat reminds Tobias of his egoism and indifference. He preferred to have the cat destroyed than to suffer in his vanity.

In the midst of the spell which the story has cast, Edna and Harry make their startling appearance. The juxtaposition of events cannot be ignored: the story of the cat is the "text"—the larger action, the explication or lesson.

A number of analogies, in fact, suggest themselves. In his relationship with Julia, Tobias takes on the characteristics of the cat; the same relationship is evident in his attitude toward Agnes. With Harry, Tobias is forced to live through the traumatic reversal again: he cannot bring himself to give the trust and love demanded by friendship. On a most profound though secret level of logic, the cat was justified; in his confrontation with Harry, Tobias finally begins to understand something of the mysterious motivations which prompted the cat to

act as she did. Love should, *must* inspire a return of
love: that's what Dante's Francesca says to justify her
adulterous love of Paolo. On that level of "higher"
morality, Tobias's cat obviously failed him. But hasn't
Tobias failed Agnes according to that same rule—and
doesn't he now fail Harry in the same way? Detached
and unfeeling (unlike Francesca), the cat was ready to
lash out at Tobias—but Tobias, as husband and
friend, has been just as guilty and just as cruel. Agnes
has forgiven him, we know; and Harry says he understands. But Tobias himself neither forgives nor understands himself—just as he could not understand the cat.

> She and I had lived together and been, well, you know,
> friends, and . . . there was no *reason*. And I hated her for
> that. I hated her, well, I suppose because I was being
> accused of something, of . . . failing. But I hadn't been
> cruel, by design; if I'd been neglectful, well, my life was
> . . . I resented it. I resented having a . . . being judged.
> Being betrayed.

Even now, he is not being cruel by design, but the effect
is exactly as if he had been. It is the silent judgment he
cannot abide; instinctively, he knows he has betrayed
his friends.

Tobias's analysis of the cat's reversal of feeling is
precise and devastating, for it applies transparently to
his own behavior toward those who love him. The appearance of Harry and Edna, who force their friendship
to a test, provides the detailed gloss to the story of the
cat. Their impossible demands—like his insistence that
the cat return his affection—drive Tobias to impotent
fury against himself. Harry has a right to insist on his
due—a true friend is ready for anything, or should be—
but Tobias can only lash out in frustration, as the cat
had. "Do you *want* us here, Tobias?" Harry insists; and
Tobias can only repeat, "You *came* here." Harry in-

stinctively understands; habit and good breeding will heal the breach; but Tobias can't stop there. He has recognized the old test. The moment is full of ironic justice. He insists on Harry's taking what is rightfully his: "YES! OF COURSE! I WANT YOU HERE! I HAVE BUILT THIS HOUSE! I WANT YOU IN IT! I WANT YOUR PLAGUE! YOU'VE GOT SOME TERROR WITH YOU? BRING IT IN!" What he really feels doesn't matter. "DON'T WE LOVE EACH OTHER?" he asks miserably, hoping that Harry will take what he *can* give and not ask the impossible of him.

> I DON'T WANT YOU HERE!
> YOU ASKED?!
> NO! I DON'T
>
> BUT BY CHRIST YOU'RE GOING TO
> STAY HERE!
> YOU'VE GOT THE RIGHT!
> THE RIGHT!

Tobias is ready to make good on a forty-year friendship. He insists on it with the same passionate energy he expended on the cat.

> BY GOD YOU'RE GOING TO TAKE IT!
> TAKE IT!
> DO YOU HEAR ME?!
> YOU BRING YOUR TERROR AND YOU COME IN
>   HERE AND YOU LIVE WITH US!
> YOU BRING YOUR PLAGUE!
> YOU STAY WITH US!
> I DON'T WANT YOU HERE!
> I DON'T LOVE YOU!
> BUT BY GOD . . . YOU STAY!

Harry, like the cat, recognizes the imposition and refuses Tobias's offer. Love should be spontaneous and generous, make no demands or conditions. Tobias has failed the test again; and Harry gracefully withdraws.

The solution is less dramatic than the painful separation of *The Zoo Story* or the sacrifice of *Tiny Alice*, but just as terrible. In abdicating his responsibility, Tobias withdraws into frustrated loneliness. "I tried," he says when it is all over, "I was honest." He has settled for the illusion of peace. The ordeal, the Terror, is reduced to conventional proportions and buried with all the other failures of the past. Honesty has come and gone, and Tobias is once more in the limbo of the impotent with Clare and Julia. He has survived the Terror, but defeat will continue to plague him.

It is Agnes who quietly and efficiently takes command when the shouting is over, easing Tobias into the old detachment, the quiet routine which he craves. Agnes provides the clues to the interpretation of events. Her opening allusion to madness gives us the theme in its simplest form. Sanity is the necessity imposed on her. She accepts the world as defined by the others around her, not because she really prefers it that way, but because she truly loves and is prepared to give what they need. Her deceptive calm is an act of sheer will—the painful equilibrium between a Dionysian abandonment and an Apollonian restraint. She forces others to hold their own: Clare must fight back if she is to retain her identity; Julia must be scolded and comforted alternately; Tobias must be spared the emotional demands he cannot fulfill. She molds their lives into a predictable routine, reducing even the vices of the household to familiar "cliché" excesses.

Tobias is the only real challenge. What she does for Clare and Julia is unquestioned habit; but she can never take Tobias for granted or respond to his needs automatically. In her relationship with Tobias, she displays exquisite tact. Even her desperate appeal to his family responsibility, at the crucial moment when Terror threatens to move in, is full of loving tenderness. She doesn't challenge Tobias's professed love for his friends, although she recognizes it as a sentimental abstraction; she never resorts to bitterness or irony, although she has good reason to; she never takes advantage of the situation at the expense of Tobias's dignity. In spite of her quicker instincts and her better judgment, she insists that Tobias make the decision regarding Harry and Edna —convention demands it and psychological necessity dictates it. Here, as in the past, she is ready to accept whatever he decides. Her own preferences don't matter.

What she does is marshal the relevant facts for Tobias's benefit. The decision cannot be based on sentimentality or personal feeling. Tobias is not alone; the health of the entire household is at stake. Clare might survive the "invasion" ("the walking wounded often are, the least susceptible"), but what of Julia? What about Tobias himself? She sums up the case with a genial analogy:

> Let me tell you something about disease . . . mortal illness; you either are immune to it . . . or you fight it. If you are immune, you wade right in, you treat the patient until he either lives, or dies of it. But if you are *not* immune, you risk infection. Ten centuries ago—and even less—the treatment was quite simple . . . burn them. Burn their bodies, burn their houses, burn their clothes—and move to another town, if you were enlightened. But now, with modern medicine, we merely isolate; we quarantine, we ostracize—if we are not immune ourselves, or unless we are saints. So, your night-long vigil, darling, your reasoning in the cold, pure hours, has been over the patient, and not the illness. It is not Edna and Harry who have come to us—our friends—it is a disease.

Neither inertia nor grand gestures will solve the problem, cure the disease. If the others are immune, there is nothing to fear. Edna and Harry can stay as long as they wish. But if Julia and Clare and Tobias and Agnes are not immune, then they must get rid of the disease, the Terror—unless they are all prepared to be destroyed by it. Agnes is willing to take the risk of infection: "We're bound to die of something . . . soon, or in a while. Or shall we burn them out, rid ourselves of it all . . . and wait for the next invasion." But Tobias is neither Jerry nor Brother Julian. He has already made his choice; he has long since "isolated" those suffering from the disease. He has never waded in. In his own emotional life, Clare, Julia, and Agnes have been effectively quarantined. His solution to the Terror is perfectly consistent with everything else he has ever done.

Tobias is neither immune nor endowed with sainthood. His protestations of loyalty and friendship are mere bravado, though he means well. The choice Agnes has put to him so dramatically is an academic one; she knows perfectly well what Tobias will do. Agnes has already gone through the worst; nothing can either surprise or disappoint her. She, of all the members of the household, is "immune."

Agnes is the subtle chorus of the play, expanding and reinforcing Clare's oracular flashes of insight. But she is by no means detached from the action around her. The demands on her are all too real; she cannot indulge in indifference or in self-righteous sentimentality. It is up to her to keep things in check, to keep her world from falling apart. The little daily crises are safety valves which keep her from "drifting"off. She is the strongest person in the play—not because she is inspired or clairvoyant, but because she simply is dependable. Like Captain McWhirr in Conrad's *Typhoon,* she lives through the Terror because of sheer constancy and habit. Like a Dürer *Melencolia,* she has taken on the job of creating order, molding reality into an illusion of peace. She is the restrained power of love turned into

Pirandellian strength of will. She has no choice, for love too is a kind of disease and demands certain labors and cares. Tobias must be guided through his dilemma in a way that will not destroy him. Agnes is not domineering Mommy, but a wise Martha. She cannot indulge in Tobias's withdrawal into religious metaphors: "The inn is full—it's rather . . . Godlike, if I may presume: to look at it all, reconstruct, with such . . . de*tach*ment, see your*self*, you, Julia . . . Look at it all . . . play it out again, watch." But his role, Agnes reminds him, cannot be that of an observer. He must direct the action, tell others what to do. "We don't decide the route," says Agnes, speaking as representative of the "dependent" family. As such, she can only implement his decision.

> The reins we hold! It's a team of twenty horses, and we sit there, and we watch the road and check the leather . . . if our . . . man is so disposed. But there are things we do not do.

The decisions, in fact, have always been made by Tobias. It's his prerogative and duty. It was Tobias who decided they would not have another child, after their son's death. It was Tobias who decided that he and Agnes must not live as man and wife for fear of the intimacy which such a relationship would demand of him and which he was no longer disposed to give. It was Tobias who forced her slowly into a sterile life, taking to his "own sweet room" to avoid all temptation and silent recriminations. It was Tobias who allowed Julia to slide. It was Tobias who accepted Clare into the select circle of disillusioned human beings, as a kind of buffer between himself and Agnes. In all these decisions, Agnes accepted the "route" and helped him to his destination.

Agnes's will is strong, but not independent. Her task is to prod Tobias into articulating what he has already deep inside him. In her impact on Tobias, she—with

Clare and Julia—resembles the witches in *Macbeth*—
an image which Tobias himself hits on: "you'll all sit
down and watch me carefully; smoke your pipes and
stir the cauldron; watch." Clare in her demonic and
vicious sparring, Julia in her fits of temper, Agnes in her
restrained madness, mirror Tobias's own confusion.
In them, his contradictory motives take demonic shape
and assume demonic purpose. Like the witches in
Shakespeare's play, they reflect those insights he would
prefer not to acknowledge in himself. What Tobias does,
in the end, like Macbeth, is truly and completely his
own doing; the three women—like oracular apparitions
—simply forge the moment of choice, trimming away
all irrelevancies and excuses. Agnes, Clare, and Julia
give Tobias the demonic courage he needs to assume
the burden of decision and reveal himself in his true
weakness. They are squeezed together, all of them, in a
mysterious vise:

> Not even separation; that is taken care of, and in life: the
> gradual . . . demise of intensity, the private occupations,
> the substitutions. We become allegorical, my darling
> Tobias, as we grow older. The individuality we hold so
> dearly sinks into crotchet; we see ourselves by those we
> bring into it all, either by mirror or rejection, honor or
> fault.

In the trio of women, Tobias has constantly before him
the frustrated resolutions of his egoism. In them he
lives out his insufficiencies, the defects of his will.
They are the voices of his conscience, his potential
vices, and his inner madness. Like Macbeth, he would
like to think of them as *causes* driving him into action—
but the truth is that they really echo his perverted hopes.
They are not external forces, but his own disguised intentions; not the ugliness outside him, but his own
paralyzing limitations.

The beauty of the play lies in the realistic treatment of

these subtle but powerful suggestions. There is little here of the immediate, palpable mystery of *Tiny Alice* or of the shattering psychological tensions of *Who's Afraid of Virginia Woolf?* From the very beginning, *A Delicate Balance* insists on "normality"—but it is the "normality" which results from a dynamic equilibrium of forces subdued and held in check. The unruffled surface is the draining of emotion; the entire play, a sustained metaphor.

To stop at a literal or obvious meaning (a play about the vices of suburbia or about the excesses of a materialistic society) is like summing up *Macbeth* as the story of a man who kills his king in order to take over the throne. Beyond the facts of the story, in both, is the struggle to transform reality into the image of the will. Where the will is corrupt or uncertain, it will project corruption and uncertainty. Tobias, like Macbeth, nurtures certain private ambitions, but he cannot articulate them as creatures of his will—and when they are finally given shape, he does not acknowledge them at once, hoping to trammel up the consequences if possible, jump the peace to come for the serenity of here and now. His partner in weakness—like Macbeth's partner in greatness—has dedicated her energies to helping him accomplish his ends. But Agnes, like Lady Macbeth, can go only so far. At the heart of darkness, Tobias—like Shakespeare's hero—must stand alone to face the terror of the completed deed. In Tobias, we catch a glimpse of the destructive Gorgon which turns love and trust into madness. In Agnes, we have a candid statement of its potential threat; but unlike Lady Macbeth, Agnes wins the battle against demonic heroism.

The action of the play moves from symbol to explication in a series of ever-growing circles of meaning, which is Albee's characteristic approach to dramatic exposition. Out of this dialectic—the kaleidoscopic superimposition of intention and result, statement and insight, truth and paradox—comes the illusion of reality, which is always a delicate balance of literal and metaphorical, familiar particulars and poetic image.

Albee's later play, *All Over*, presents a set of characters at once reminiscent of the people in *A Delicate Balance*, but the play as a whole is more static and less suggestive. The clichés are unrelieved and remain mere statements, the bursts of energy are less convincing dramatically, the characters less interesting in themselves. Perhaps *All Over* falls short of perfection as we have come to define it in Albee's art. The dialogue might indeed have been sharper, the insights more revealing, the characterizations more varied; but as an extended conceit, the play must rank with the best in Albee's repertory. The living are dying just as surely as the unseen patient behind the hospital screen. They make sounds but there is no energy to sustain them; they talk of love, but there is no trace of it. *All Over* is the dying breath of an exhausted past. There is no meaningful future ahead, only the heightened immediacy of the present moment—a present which is gloomy and inarticulate, buried in self-pity and isolated intentions, as artificial as the temporary illusion of life provided by tubes, injections, and medication. In final analysis, this monotonous, subdued skirting of psychological realities may have been exactly what the dramatist intended; the death vigil is the unmistakable sign of impotence. It is an obvious sign, like the conventions of medieval moralities, but no less forceful because of its obvious nature. In this context—as a conceit of dramatic realism —*All Over* is provocative theater.

6

Partita
Box and *Quotations from Chairman Mao Tse-Tung*

> *False hopes, false dreams, false masks and modes of youth.*
> *The City of Dreadful Night*

In a repertory of inventive and unique dramatic experiences, *Box* and *Quotations from Chairman Mao Tse-Tung* must stand alone as the most ingenious product of Albee's fertile imagination. Whether or not it is (or they are, together) a full-length play remains open to question; and its structure and form may be hard to define, even in the avant-garde terms which have been evolved thus far. It is a leap into the unexplored, a Platonic "recognition," an experience altogether new and yet—characteristically—curiously reminiscent of earlier works of Albee's as also of dramatic patterns of other ages.

Up to this point, Albee has adhered to the conventions of dramatic action as an ordering of events in time—conventions which have been stretched almost to the limits of communicability and which have opened up new and exciting possibilities for our theater. The very notion of *time* has been tried and tested in a number of interesting ways, from *realistic sequence* (*The Zoo Story, The Death of Bessie Smith, Who's Afraid of Virginia Woolf?, A Delicate Balance*) to *allegorical present* (*The Sandbox, The American Dream*) and *inversion* or Sophoclean confounding of past and present (*Tiny Alice*). In *Box* dramatic action becomes for the first time a reduction of time to a spectrum of *absolute moments*, each reflecting a completed cycle or lifetime. There is no dramatic situation or setting as we have come to know them in other plays, no *progression;* rather, an unraveling of impressions depicted as a series of reverberations, of concentric expanding circles of meaning, repetitions of an eternal present. Each protagonist is revealed in his characteristic posture; each betrays in the irresistible urge to indulge in his precious scraps of vanity, the nature of his *will.*

Two curious features accompany this handling of dramatic action as independent vectors of will. One is the abstract anagogical statement of meaning in *Box,* expanded—as variations—in *Quotations,* where—at a given moment—the disembodied Voice of *Box* is heard again in a kind of refrain, illuminating by the sheer juxtaposition of lines already heard the meaning of the various separate monologues. The second interesting feature is the similarity between these protagonists and the figures of the *commedia dell'arte,* where individuality is reduced to the grossest particulars and, paradoxically, raised to *types.* In the Albee play (for this writer, the two are definitely one single experience), names remain generic and remind us of an earlier combination— *The Sandbox* and *The American Dream.* The parallel is worth noting. In both cases, the two plays are interrelated (*Box* is a more integral unit); both pairs were written together or grew out of a single dramatic idea; both explore symbolism and allegory in a direct, almost skeletal fashion; both rely on representative types, minimizing action as plot. The most significant difference is that, in the earlier combination, the protagonists are near-perfect personifications, while *Box* depicts universal figures through well-defined particulars, exactly in the manner of the *commedia dell'arte*. Long-Winded Lady has features reminiscent of some of Albee's earlier women, including Mommy and Grandma; but like the other characters in *Box*, she is real in a way that Mommy and Grandma and Mrs. Barker in themselves are not.

Mao, after all, is Mao; and Long-Winded Lady—in spite of her generic name—is very carefully detailed as a human being. She is a subdued Martha who has lived through the frustrations of both Agnes and Miss Alice, an articulate reminder of female instinct and self-indulgence spelled out in incidents at once unique and typical. Old Woman is the embodiment of social and personal complaints in a Brechtian vein, but the Brechtian social premise has been altogether reversed in a devastating critique. Minister could be any one of many chosen at random, but he is perfectly captured as an individual in his own right, whose way of life is a *reductio ad absurdum*, a paradoxical dramatic statement without words. In Minister, Albee has gone further than ever before in reducing the multiplicity of personality to characteristic *pose* articulated as *gestures*, straining to their utmost the dramatic possibilities of characterization.

The Box—like the giant replica in *Tiny Alice*—is visual symbolism at its best, which is to say, completely transparent. But here too Albee has moved forward; the transparent symbolism of the Box as the world or universe is of the same kind as that of the replica in *Tiny Alice*—both suggest the larger anagogical dimension outside of time—but the Box actually becomes transparent in the course of the play, easing us back gradually into *allegorical time* (the deck of a moving ocean liner suggesting the familiar cliché of the journey through life) and dissolving the here and now, at the end, with the reappearance of the Box and—paradoxically—the contrapuntal enriching of the dialogue with the reintroduction of Voice.

The play is literally encased in eternity. We seem to be inside the replica of *Tiny Alice,* in the giant memory of history; and Alice herself has become audible in her own domain as the invisible commentator of the past. Time itself has ceased to be a progression and has become an absolute. The protagonists of *Quotations* are the varieties of total experience, each trapped in his own consciousness (or box). Minister alone reaches out helplessly every so often, as though to communicate something to Long-Winded Lady, but he never speaks. The separate monologues are related by echoing lines, recurring words, or the tail end of a fleeting idea. Together, the four protagonists of *Quotations* provide a musical partita, refractions of the single eternal Voice, parodies of Its absolute self-sufficiency, echoes in particular terms of Its search for meaningful absolute statement.

Voice is the oracle; the others constitute a kind of chorus struggling to find relevancy and truth in what reaches them of the eternal insight into things. Each of the protagonists in *Quotations* tries in his own way to solve the puzzle of order as suggested by the disembodied Voice. In the end, the single Voice returns—unchanged, unimpressed, impassive. Like the waters of the sea remembered by Long-Winded Lady, It covers over human sounds (the long sequence of the woman's falling into the ocean is a suggestive image of the larger text); memory empties out, multiplicity is reduced once more to pristine, bare unity. Even the revolutionary optimism of Mao—like Dante's vision of the busy world from the perspective of eternity—seems puny and unreal.

Mao dominates the scene in terms of explicit statement. He alone of the four seems to know where he's going, what he wants; he alone seems confident of his purpose. He is completely wrapped up in it, an unquestioning believer in precepts which he repeats with computerlike precision. He is the perfect dramatic contrast to Long-Winded Lady, who is intimately preoccupied with the details of her life, intensely and pathetically unsure of her purpose, completely self-involved in her suffering, the articulate voice of the existential agony of *dying*, for whom death is meaningless since she has nothing to die *for*. Mao, according to his avowed commitment, has everything to die for.

On a profounder level, this contrast turns into an enigma. Long-Winded Lady is, ultimately, the most interesting and most human of the four separate distinct voices. She is also the most truthful, for her agony is the reality about the human condition. Mao, in these terms, becomes a mere robot. His optimism sounds empty after a while; his hopes seem naïve and simplistic. He is also the most indifferent, the least aware of the four. His rhetoric is that of the preacher who has failed to grasp the human dilemma.

What is truly genial about all this is the intensely *human* feeling Albee manages to evoke in this most farfetched of his allegorical compositions. A quick comparison with earlier American plays in this genre, *The Skin of Our Teeth* or *Camino Real*, or, more recently, with something like Ionesco's *The Bald Soprano* dramatizes the difference. In *Box* abstractions never become personifications or generalizations, but retain from beginning to end distinct shape and form, personality, particulars which define the substance of individuality. Minister is as finely drawn in his having "nothing to say" as any of the Dantesque figures caught in their everlasting virtue or vice. Long-Winded Lady and Old Woman come from very different backgrounds, each distinct and recognizable, each voicing her own personal disappoint-

ments, shocks, vulnerabilities, pathetic dreams. Mao
is reduced to the sounds of rhetoric, and Minister is
nothing but the *gestures* of rhetoric—but both are perfectly themselves with all the idiosyncrasies of their
particular public image. Together, these four constitute
a graduated insight into chaos, each holding on to his
and her own vestige of order—personal memories,
slogans, lessons and precepts, emotions shared with
others—each contributing to the final resolution of tension to tonic.

Order is the absolute for which the characters search
vainly in the memory; Voice reviews it in its many diversified forms, while the others project it against their own
personal histories, giving it explicit content. For Mao it
is simple and straightforward: order is the triumph of
good over evil. The terms are unambiguous: capitalism
is bad, but it has managed to win control; communism
is good and therefore has a responsibility to correct
the greed of the wealthy. The upsetting of the status quo
in which capitalism dominates will be bloody, but it is
necessary. The cunning of history has been harnessed
by the good forces to accomplish political revolution, the
means which will bring about the desired millennium.

But Mao's manner of spouting slogans belies an inability to convert. The others seem not to hear him at
all; and although Long-Winded Lady and Old Woman
seem all intent on their own problems, in the same way,
the audience reacts to their compelling narratives much
more spontaneously than they do to Mao's impersonal
political insights. Whether what he says is true or not
is irrelevant in Albee's design; what matters is the contrast drawn between the hopes articulated by Mao and
his almost inhuman manner of setting them forth. He
professes humanitarian concern, but is absolutely deaf
to the agonizing self-examination of the others; his is an
arrogant optimism which—like the ambitious systems of

the great philosophers in Dante's hell—will never come to rest.

Mao's optimism is, within the context of the play, a frustrated hope, similar to the frustrated hopes of all the others around him. He is caught, as it were, in the summing up of his philosophy—and that summing up is a future that comes into being only by "withering away." The communist consummation in this scheme is just as abstract as the Christian heaven: both are outside human experience, both are projections of faith, both are doomed to what might-have-been or ought-to-be. Mao is the voice of political utopias, faithful to the end, but with a rhetoric of purpose that wrecks its very convictions.

For Old Woman, order is filial duty, family obligations, unquestioned love and unchanging affection, the private utopia, the personal dream never to be fulfilled. For Long-Winded Lady, order is meaningful cause-and-effect, rational explanations for irrational events, virtue and stoicism rewarded. She is the most sophisticated of the four. In Albee's dramatic repertory, she is the culmination of a long line of domineering women, tempered by age and experience into articulate resignation. She is a careful observer of human nature, ruthless in estimating her own impulses as well as those of others, uncompromising in her judgments, understanding but helpless in the face of suffering, isolated in the meaningless trap of life.

For Minister, order is divine compassion and sacrifice, that sympathetic identification which can change another person's life: Christ-like giving. But Minister never succeeds in completing his empty gestures; he falls short of genuine communication. He, most of all, is helpless.

All these parts of personality, boxed in themselves, together, hope for order where there is none, dream of reconstructing the past into the perfect image which the memory retains. Each is isolated from the others, but together they produce a harmonious whole. Old Woman's narrative is a ballad full of ironies and insistent refrains which keep going back to the wounds inflicted on her by her children. There is something almost grotesque about her rigorous control of rhyme and rhythm, her easy vernacular and vulgarisms—the form sets up a nervous tension with the content. The pathos of the desertion she must suffer in her helpless old age is never quite pathetic. In its predictable tempo, this narrative sets a kind of musical mood, against which Long-Winded Lady's sober and poetic flights are heard like the rise and fall of the sea gulls. Instead of rhyme and rhythm, we have a series of disjointed, staccato images, long passages of nostalgic reminiscences deflated at intervals by electrifying thrusts of irony or irrepressible cries of disappointment. The two voices complement one another as vulgar and sophisticated expressions of the same basic frustrations. Mao, like a constant musical burden, provides the heavy base from which the vivid humanity of the women rises in its straining toward melodic resolution. His is the monotony of deep chords. Minister punctuates and phrases, sets the pitch and tonalities, the intensity of the volume. He is indispensable in keeping track of musical time and directing, in his gestures, the partita.

Time, in its philosophical sense, is the completed eternal *now*. Yet, even more interesting, is the recurring suggestion (again very Dantesque) that *now* is the painful memory of what might have been. But Albee's is not a providential universe. What might have been is simply the naïve memory playing tricks. The past is available to each of the four protagonists as fragments, bits and pieces which they try desperately to reconstruct into a meaningful pattern. There is no before or after, no sequence, no cause-and-effect relationship which could salvage the painful scraps of purpose now recalled. Long-Winded Lady remembers having broken her thumb as a child and how the pain set in only when she willed it, when she accepted the word and idea from others. She willed pain before she actually experienced any physical sensation. Direction and purpose, like time, are constantly reversed, often reduced to the irrational and instinctive. Falling into the sea is a falling *up*.

The Box itself, though "nicely done," "well put . . . together," is an empty distorted cube, until the memory furnishes it with its own pathetic images and shapes. Like Grandma's boxes in *The American Dream*, it gradually accumulates all the frustrated dreams, fictions, fears, deceptions, terrors of those who find themselves in possession of it. In the end, it emerges as the repository of history—but a history which, like the events and memories of the four protagonists, cannot be reconstructed meaningfully. There is no *reason* in it, no teleology operating to define progression and salvation. History is the accumulated disasters of mankind, the irrational cruelties and sufferings immortalized in the memory and heightened through art. When art begins to hurt, then the corruption is complete. History is the chaos of hell; beauty is loss. In the memory of History, in Voice, there is infinite sadness, the sadness of a distant Fate watching its heroes fight valiantly in their meaningless battles with life.

Time cannot exist, for it too is just a memory. Small cracks and large deaths produce Platonic recall, death and dying are contradictory facts, communist ideology and the humanitarian pronouncements of the Pope are somehow the same. The juxtaposition of unrelated and contradictory events sometimes finds expression in art, but the meaning of art is itself a paradox, "not what is familiar, necessarily, but order . . . on its own terms."

Art begins with the hurt which comes as a result of that awareness. "When art begins to hurt, it's time to look around." But in looking around, time dissolves into the old fragments, the old flashes which are gone before they can be grasped. The experience heightens observation: sounds are remembered which were never heard; the fog, never actually seen, takes shape before our eyes; the unfamiliar *tonic* is recognized in the tension. Art is the insight into painful memory, the moment when order flashes on us like divine prescience, without warning, touching us with beauty and loss.

The statements about art are the most provocative in the play. They provide a warning and a clue. Action, characterization, dialogue, theme, setting, and form generally are in themselves internally consistent, but their consistency can only be grasped as a recognition of truths never fully articulated. Albee himself, in the introduction to the plays, suggests the kind of reaction his audience should experience. The two works are "quite simple," he insists—

> By that I mean that while technically they are fairly complex and they do demand from an audience quite close attention, their content can be apprehended without much difficulty. All that one need do is—quite simply—relax and let the plays happen. That, and be willing to approach the dramatic experience without a preconception of what the nature of the dramatic experience should be.

Art must move or wither, and the audience must be willing "to experience a work on its own terms." Albee ably directs his audience toward this end. Juxtaposition, verbal echoes, seemingly farfetched analogies, allegorical transparencies, profound insights contained in memorable images—the very substance of his dramatic fluency and the mark of his *simplicity* as a playwright—are used here with the ease of musical genius.

The critic himself may be at a loss as to how to order

his impressions of these remarkable plays into the familiar patterns of critical appraisal. Albee has little patience with critics; and no doubt he is right in suggesting that very often critics confuse audiences with their "explanations." Still, the temptation to analyze and explain is irresistible. In dealing with the two plays here discussed, the temptation and the dangers are especially strong. One is tempted to summarize the superb artistry and the profound insights of *Box* and *Quotations from Chairman Mao Tse-Tung* in Albee's own idiom—for it's not what the thing itself says but what you say to yourself when you hear it . . . the resolution you make to tonic, when you hear the tense chord—from tension to tonic.

You see it hit the water beyond earshot and you say, or you hear yourself say, "plut."

You *hear* about bell buoys and sea gulls and feel as if you'd actually felt the sea fog and all the rest, which you haven't felt.

There's a pain which makes you go from one to the other, a pain that makes you expect and break through to the other.

Like, you take that minister just sitting there, with his pipe and tobacco pouch. I don't have to tell you what. . . .

But now, you tell me, you nice, broad-minded people out there, my ivy leaguers and pseudo ivy leaguers, what do you say to yourselves when you listen to my fat Mao? And what about your husband's mother-in-law, who would be no problem if . . . well, if everything were socialized . . . but, intelligently! No, it wasn't *so* bad with the three of us. We just made it bad, we knew what one says and we *made* it happen.

But what can *you* say?

What *can* I say? says the minister. Or did I say it for him?

So long as there are some with nothing we have no right to anything.

I say the United States is a falling paper tiger.

Falling up.

In a box—

If you don't hit it, it won't fall.

That's when art begins to hurt.

We give up something for something, and monsters of all kinds shall be destroyed.

Waiting in the box with the *possible* sound of it.

But was it the minister, or the old lady, or I, or the box that said, through the small cracks: "Good heavens, no; I have nothing to die for."

What I thought I heard was

Plut!

—or was it sea gulls and buoys.

Albee, Edward. *All Over*. New York: Atheneum, 1971.

———. *The American Dream and the Zoo Story*. New York: The New American Library, Signet Books, 1961.

———. *Box and Quotations from Chairman Mao Tse-Tung*. New York: Atheneum, 1969.

———. *A Delicate Balance*. New York: Atheneum, 1966.

———. Introduction to *Three Plays by Noel Coward*. New York: Dell, A Delta Book, 1965.

———. *The Sandbox, The Death of Bessie Smith, with Fam and Yam*. New York: The New American Library, Signet Books, 1960.

———. *Tiny Alice*. New York: Atheneum, 1965.

———. *Who's Afraid of Virginia Woolf?*. New York: Atheneum, 1964.

Amacher, Richard E. *Edward Albee*. New York: Twayne Publishers, 1969.

Baxandall, Lee. "The Theatre of Edward Albee," *Tulane Drama Review*, 9, No. 4 (1965), 19–40.

Caputi, Anthony, ed. *Modern Drama*. New York: W. W. Norton, 1966.

Curry, Ryder Hector and Michael Porte. "The Surprising Unconscious of Edward Albee," *Drama Survey*, 7, Nos. 1–2 [Double Issue] (1968–1969), 59–68.

Debusscher, Gilbert. *Edward Albee: Tradition and Renewal*, trans. Anne D. Williams. Brussels: Center for American Studies, 1969.

Downer, Alan S., ed. *American Drama and its Critics*. Chicago: University of Chicago Press, 1965.

————. *Recent American Drama.* Minneapolis: University of Minnesota Press, 1961.

Esslin, Martin. *The Theatre of the Absurd.* New York: Doubleday, Anchor Books, 1961.

Gassner, John. *The Theatre in Our Times.* New York: Crown Publishers, 1954.

Goldstone, Richard, ed. *Contexts of the Drama.* New York: McGraw-Hill, 1968.

Hogan, Robert. *Arthur Miller.* Minneapolis: University of Minnesota Press, 1964.

Ionesco, Eugene. *Notes and Counter Notes,* trans. Donald Watson. New York: Grove Press, 1964.

Paolucci, Anne, trans. "Introduction to the Italian Theater, by Luigi Pirandello," in *Genius of the Italian Theater,* ed. Eric Bentley. New York: The New American Library, Mentor Books, 1964.

Rutenberg, Michael E. *Edward Albee: Playwright in Protest.* New York: Avon, Discus Books, 1969.

Willeford, William. "The Mouse in the Model," *Modern Drama,* 12, September 1969, 135–45.

Index